Informing the legislative debate since 1914

Financial Services and General Government (FSGG): FY2014 Appropriations

Baird Webel, Coordinator
Specialist in Financial Economics

January 7, 2014

Congressional Research Service

7-5700

www.crs.gov

R43352

Summary

The Financial Services and General Government (FSGG) appropriations bill provides funding for the Department of the Treasury, the Executive Office of the President (EOP), the judiciary, the District of Columbia, and more than two dozen independent agencies. Among those independent agencies are the General Services Administration (GSA), the Office of Personnel Management (OPM), the Small Business Administration (SBA), the Securities and Exchange Commission (SEC), and the United States Postal Service (USPS). The Commodity Futures Trading Commission (CFTC) is funded in the House through the Agriculture appropriations bill and in the Senate through the FSGG bill. CFTC funding is included in all FSGG funding tables in this report.

On April 10, 2013, President Obama submitted his FY2014 budget request. The request included a total of $45.4 billion for agencies funded through the FSGG appropriations bill, including $315 million for the CFTC.

On July 23, 2013, the House Committee on Appropriations reported H.R. 2786, the Financial Services and General Government Appropriations Act, 2014. H.R. 2786 would provide $38.1 billion for agencies funded through the House FSGG Appropriations Subcommittee. In addition, the CFTC would receive $194.6 million through the FY2014 Agriculture appropriations bill (H.R. 2410). Total FY2014 funding provided by the House would be $38.3 billion, about $7.1 billion below the President's FY2014 request.

On July 25, 2013, the Senate Appropriations Committee reported its FY2013 financial services bill, S. 1371. The Senate committee's bill would provide $44.3 billion for FSGG agencies, including $315 million for the CFTC, for FY2014, which would be $1.1 billion below the President's FY2014 request.

Because none of the 12 regular appropriations bills for FY2014 was enacted prior to the beginning of the fiscal year, a funding gap commenced on October 1, 2013. On October 16, 2013, the Senate passed a previously passed House bill, H.R. 2775, with an amendment that, in part, provided interim continuing appropriations for the previous fiscal year's projects and activities and retitled H.R. 2775 as the Continuing Appropriations Act, 2014. Later that same day, the House agreed to the Senate amendment to H.R. 2775. H.R. 2775 was signed into law on October 17, 2013 (P.L. 113-46), thus terminating the funding gap that same day. With some routine exceptions, P.L. 113-46 provides budget authority through January 15, 2014.

Contents

Tables

Contacts

Most Recent Developments

On April 10, 2013, President Obama submitted his FY2014 budget request.[1] The request included a total of $45.4 billion for agencies funded through the Financial Services and General Government (FSGG) appropriations bill, including $315 million for the Commodity Futures Trading Commission (CFTC).[2]

On July 23, 2013, the House Committee on Appropriations (hereafter "the House committee") reported the Financial Services and General Government Appropriations Act, 2014 (H.R. 2786; H.Rept. 113-172).[3] H.R. 2786 would provide $38.1 billion for agencies funded through the House FSGG Appropriations Subcommittee. In addition, the CFTC would receive $194.6 million through the FY2014 Agriculture appropriations bill (H.R. 2410, H.Rept. 113-116[4]). Total FY2014 funding provided by the House would be $38.3 billion, about $7.1 billion below the President's FY2014 request.

On July 25, 2013, the Senate Committee on Appropriations (hereafter "the Senate committee") reported its Financial Services and General Government Appropriations Act, 2014 (S. 1371; S.Rept. 113-80).[5] S. 1371 would provide $44.3 billion for FSGG agencies, including $315 million for the CFTC, which would be $1.1 billion below the President's FY2014 request. **Table 1** reflects the status of FSGG appropriations measures at key points in the appropriations process.

Prior to the beginning of FY2014, congressional action occurred on an interim continuing resolution (CR) that would have provided continuing appropriations for projects and activities for which authority existed during the previous fiscal year.[6] H.J.Res. 59 was introduced on September 10, 2013, and passed the House on September 20. On September 27, the Senate passed H.J.Res. 59 with an amendment. Subsequent actions to resolve differences between the House and Senate, which included the consideration of various House amendments to that Senate amendment, were unsuccessful. No other interim CRs that broadly covered the previous fiscal year's projects and activities received congressional action at that time.[7]

---

[1] Office of Management and Budget, *Budget of the United States Government, Fiscal Year 2014*, (Washington, DC: GPO, 2013). In addition to the primary budget document, OMB also releases portions entitled *Analytical Perspectives*, *Historical Tables*, and *Appendix*. Citations to the primary budget document will take the form of "*Budget of the United States, FY2014,*" followed by the appropriate page number; citations to the other documents will take the form of, for example, "*Analytical Perspectives, Budget of the United States, FY2014,*" followed by page numbers. Current and past year's budget documents can be found at http://www.whitehouse.gov/omb/budget.

[2] The President does provide totals broken down by congressional appropriations bills. The $45.4 billion total is as calculated by the Senate Appropriations Committee.

[3] U.S. Congress, House Committee on Appropriations, *Financial Services and General Government Appropriations Bill, 2014*, report to accompany H.R. 2786, H.Rept. 113-172, 113th Cong., 1st sess., July 23, 2013 (Washington: GPO, 2013).

[4] U.S. Congress, House Committee on Appropriations, *Agriculture, Rural Development, Food and Drug Administration, and Related Agencies Appropriations Bill, 2014*, report to accompany H.R. 2410, H.Rept. 113-116, 113th Cong., 1st sess., June 18, 2013 (Washington: GPO, 2013).

[5] U.S. Congress, Senate Committee on Appropriations, *Financial Services and General Government Appropriations Bill, 2014*, report to accompany S. 1371, S.Rept. 113-80, 113th Cong., 1st sess., July 25, 2013 (Washington: GPO, 2013).

[6] For further information with regard to CRs, see CRS Report R42647, *Continuing Resolutions: Overview of Components and Recent Practices*, by Jessica Tollestrup.

[7] A narrow automatic continuing resolution, P.L. 113-39, was enacted on September 30 to cover FY2014 pay and (continued...)

Because none of the 12 regular appropriations bills for FY2014 were enacted prior to the beginning of the fiscal year, a funding gap commenced on October 1, 2013.[8] Congressional action on FY2014 appropriations between October 2 and October 15 was generally limited to a number of narrow CRs to provide funding for certain programs or classes of individuals.[9]

On October 16, 2013, the Senate passed a previously passed house bill, H.R. 2775, with an amendment that, in part, provided interim continuing appropriations for the previous fiscal year's projects and activities, and retitled H.R. 2775 as the Continuing Appropriations Act, 2014. Later that same day, the House agreed to the Senate amendment to H.R. 2775. The CR was signed into law on October 17, 2013 (P.L. 113-46), thus terminating the funding gap that same day. With some routine exceptions, P.L. 113-46 provided budget authority through January 15, 2014.

Under P.L. 113-46, most FSGG accounts were funded at the same level as they were for FY2013. However, there were exceptions to this general approach, which are often referred to in appropriations argot as "anomalies." The anomalies identified in P.L. 113-46 include

- Section 125 provided appropriations for "The Judiciary—Courts of Appeals, District Courts, and Other Judicial Services—Salaries and Expenses" at a rate of operations of $4,820,181,000, with an amount not to exceed $25,000,000 to be available for transfer between accounts to maintain minimum operating levels.

- Section 126 provided appropriations for "The Judiciary—Courts of Appeals, District Courts, and Other Judicial Services—Defender Services" at a rate for operations of $1,012,000,000.

- Section 127 provided that the District of Columbia may expend local funds under the heading "District of Columbia Funds" for such programs and activities under title IV of H.R. 2786 as reported by the Committee on Appropriations of the House of Representatives. The rate of spending is to be the rate set forth under "District of Columbia Funds—Summary of Expenses" as included in the Fiscal Year 2014 Budget Request Act of 2013 (D.C. Act 20-127), as modified as of the date of the enactment of this joint resolution.

(...continued)

allowances for (1) certain members of the Armed Forces, (2) certain Department of Defense (DOD) civilian personnel, and (3) other specified DOD and Department of Homeland Security contractors, during any potential funding gap that might ensue beginning on October 1 (H.R. 3210; P.L. 113-39). For further information on P.L. 113-39, see CRS Report R41948, *Automatic Continuing Resolutions: Background and Overview of Recent Proposals*, by Jessica Tollestrup.

[8] A funding gap is the interval during the fiscal year when appropriations for a particular project or activity are not enacted into law, either in the form of a regular appropriations act or a CR. For further information, see CRS Report RS20348, *Federal Funding Gaps: A Brief Overview*, by Jessica Tollestrup.

[9] These CRs include H.J.Res. 70, H.J.Res. 71, H.J.Res. 72, H.J.Res. 73, H.J.Res. 75, H.J.Res. 76, H.J.Res. 77, H.J.Res. 79, H.J.Res. 80, H.J.Res. 82, H.J.Res. 83, H.J.Res. 84, H.J.Res. 85, H.J.Res. 89, H.J.Res. 90, H.J.Res. 91, and H.R. 3230. Of these, only the Department of Defense Survivor Benefits Continuing Appropriations Resolution of 2014 (H.J.Res. 91; P.L. 113-44) was enacted into law.

Table 1. Status of FY2014 Financial Services and General Government Appropriations

Subcommittee Markup		House Report	House Passage	Senate Report	Senate Passage	Conference Report	Conference Report Adopted		Public Law
House	Senate						House	Senate	
7/10/13	7/23/13	H.Rept. 113-172 7/23/2013		S.Rept. 113-80 7/25/2013					

Overview

The House and Senate Committees on Appropriations reorganized their subcommittee structures in early 2007. Each chamber created a new Financial Services and General Government Subcommittee. In the House, the jurisdiction of the FSGG Subcommittee comprised primarily agencies that had been under the jurisdiction of the Subcommittee on Transportation, Treasury, Housing and Urban Development, the Judiciary, the District of Columbia, and Independent Agencies, commonly referred to as "TTHUD."[10] In addition, the House FSGG Subcommittee was assigned four independent agencies that had been under the jurisdiction of the Science, State, Justice, Commerce, and Related Agencies Subcommittee: the Federal Communications Commission (FCC), the Federal Trade Commission (FTC), the Securities and Exchange Commission (SEC), and the Small Business Administration (SBA).

In the Senate, the jurisdiction of the new FSGG Subcommittee was a combination of agencies from the jurisdiction of three previously existing subcommittees. The District of Columbia, which had its own subcommittee in the 109th Congress, was placed under the purview of the FSGG Subcommittee, as were four independent agencies that had been under the jurisdiction of the Commerce, Justice, Science, and Related Agencies Subcommittee: the FCC, FTC, SEC, and SBA. In addition, most of the agencies that had been under the jurisdiction of the Subcommittee on Transportation, Treasury, the Judiciary, Housing and Urban Development, and Related Agencies were assigned to the FSGG Subcommittee.[11]

As a result of this reorganization, the House and Senate FSGG Subcommittees have nearly identical jurisdictions except that the CFTC is under the jurisdiction of the FSGG Subcommittee in the Senate but not in the House, where it is under the Agriculture Subcommittee.

The FSGG appropriations bill includes funding for the Department of the Treasury, the Executive Office of the President (EOP), the judiciary, the District of Columbia, and more than two dozen independent agencies. For these five segments of the FSGG appropriations bill, **Table 2** lists the enacted amounts for FY2013 prior to the sequester under the Budget Control Act of 2011 (P.L.

---

[10] The agencies previously under the jurisdiction of the TTHUD Subcommittee that did not become part of the FSGG subcommittee were the Department of Transportation, the Department of Housing and Urban Development (HUD), the Architectural and Transportation Barriers Compliance Board, the Federal Maritime Commission, the National Transportation Safety Board, the Neighborhood Reinvestment Corporation, and the United States Interagency Council on Homelessness.

[11] The agencies that did not transfer from TTHUD to FSGG were Transportation, HUD, the Architectural and Transportation Barriers Compliance Board, the Federal Maritime Commission, the National Transportation Safety Board, the Neighborhood Reinvestment Corporation, and the United States Interagency Council on Homelessness.

112-25), the President's FY2014 request, and amounts recommended by the House and Senate appropriations committees for FY2014.

Note on FY2013 and Sequestration

Past Congressional Research Service (CRS) reports on FSGG appropriations have carried detailed comparisons with previous years' funding levels. Due to the impact of sequestration on budget authority available to the federal government under the Consolidated and Further Continuing Appropriations Act, 2013 (P.L. 113-6) and the Disaster Relief Appropriations Act, 2013 (P.L. 113-2), complete post-sequestration numbers are not available at the program, project, and activity levels. Therefore, the charts in this report generally contain information on only pre-sequester funding levels for FY2013 as reported by the Senate Committee on Appropriations.[12] In some cases, particularly with regard to funding for the Treasury, CRS was supplied post-sequester numbers by the executive branch and **Table 3** includes these figures.

Table 2. Financial Services and General Government Appropriations, FY2013-FY2014

(in millions of dollars)

Agency	FY2013 Pre-sequester	FY2014 Request	FY2014 House Committee	FY2014 Senate Committee	FY2014 Enacted
Department of the Treasury	$12,196	$13,229	$9,044	$12,203	
Executive Office of the President	669	623	625	679	
The Judiciary	6,998	7,222	7,029	7,162	
District of Columbia	674	676	636	675	
Independent Agencies	22,809	23,685	20,943	23,585	
Total	**$43,346**	**$45,435**	**$38,277**	**$44,304**	

Sources: H.Rept. 113-172; S.Rept. 113-180; and H.Rept. 113-116.

Notes: Totals for each column include funding for the Commodity Futures Trading Commission. The CFTC is funded in the House through the Agriculture appropriations bill and in the Senate through the Financial Services and General Government bill. Figures include rescissions and offsetting collections. Totals may not sum due to rounding. "Pre-sequester FY2013" figures are from S.Rept. 113-80 and include across-the-board cuts under the Consolidated and Further Continuing Appropriations Act, 2013 (P.L. 113-6). The House bill funds some mandatory spending for the President, the judiciary, and the independent agencies in Title VI while the Senate bill includes this spending in Titles II, III, and V, respectively.

The Department of the Treasury[13]

This section examines FY2014 appropriations for the Treasury Department and its operating bureaus, including the Internal Revenue Service (IRS). The Treasury Department performs a

---

[12] Data from the Senate report is used because it is more recent and includes the across-the-board cuts included in P.L. 113-6.

[13] This section authored by Gary Guenther (x7-7742).

variety of critical functions. They include protecting the nation's financial system against a variety of illicit activities (particularly money laundering and terrorist financing), collecting tax revenue and enforcing tax laws, managing and accounting for federal debt, administering the federal government's finances, regulating financial institutions, and producing and distributing coins and currency.

Brief Summary of the Treasury's Structure and Functions

At its most basic level of organization, Treasury consists of departmental offices and operating bureaus. In general, the offices are responsible for formulating and implementing policy and managing Treasury's operations, while the bureaus undertake specific tasks assigned to Treasury, mainly through statutory mandates. In the past decade or so, the bureaus have accounted for more than 95% of the agency's funding and workforce.

With one exception, the bureaus and offices can be divided into those engaged in financial management and regulation and those engaged in law enforcement. In recent decades, the Comptroller of the Currency, U.S. Mint, Bureau of Engraving and Printing, Financial Management Service, Bureau of the Public Debt, and Community Development Financial Institutions Fund have been responsible for the management of the federal government's finances or the supervision and regulation of the U.S. financial system. In contrast, law enforcement has been central to the duties handled by the Alcohol and Tobacco Tax and Trade Bureau, Financial Crimes Enforcement Network, and the Treasury Forfeiture Fund. (With the advent of the Department of Homeland Security in 2002, Treasury's direct involvement in law enforcement shrank considerably.) The exception to this dichotomy is the IRS, whose main responsibilities encompass the collection of tax revenue and the enforcement of tax laws and regulations.

The operating budgets for most Treasury bureaus and offices are largely funded through annual discretionary appropriations. This certainly is the case for the IRS, Financial Management Service, Bureau of Public Debt, Financial Crimes Enforcement Network, Alcohol and Tobacco Tax and Trade Bureau, Office of the Inspector General, Treasury Inspector General for Tax Administration, Special Inspector General for the Troubled Asset Relief Program, and Community Development Financial Institutions Fund. Descriptions of these bureaus and offices follow below. By contrast, funding for the Treasury Franchise Fund, the U.S. Mint, the Bureau of Engraving and Printing, and the Office of the Comptroller of the Currency comes exclusively from the fees they receive for the services and products they provide to the public and other government agencies.

Departmental Offices

The Departmental Offices (DO) covers the salaries and other expenses of offices in the department that formulate and implement policies in the areas of domestic and international finance, terrorist financing and other financial crimes, taxation, international trade, and the domestic economy. It also provides funding for the Treasury Department's financial and personnel management, procurement operations, and information and telecommunications systems.

Department-wide Systems and Capital Investments

The Department-wide Systems and Capital Investments (DSCIP) covers expenses related to modernizing Treasury's business processes and increasing the efficiency of its operations through investments in new technology and capital improvements.

Office of Inspector General

The Office of Inspector General (OIG) covers the salaries and other expenses related to the audits and investigations conducted by OIG staff. These evaluations are intended to promote improved efficiency and effectiveness and prevent waste, fraud, and abuse in departmental operations and programs, as well as to inform the Treasury Secretary and Congress about problems or shortcomings in those activities.

Treasury Inspector General for Tax Administration

The Treasury Inspector General for Tax Administration (TIGTA) covers salaries and other expenses related to the audits and investigations conducted by TIGTA staff. These evaluations are intended to promote greater efficiency and effectiveness in the administration of tax law, deter or prevent fraud and abuse in IRS programs and operations, and recommend changes in those activities to solve problems or remedy deficiencies.

Special Inspector General for the Troubled Asset Relief Program

The Special Inspector General for the Troubled Asset Relief Program (SIGTARP) covers salaries and other expenses related to the audits and investigations into the management and effectiveness of TARP conducted by SIGTARP staff. The office was established by the same law that created TARP: the Emergency Economic Stabilization Act.[14]

Financial Crimes Enforcement Network

The Financial Crimes Enforcement Network (FinCEN) covers salaries and other expenses related to the activities of FinCEN, whose main responsibility is to protect the domestic financial system from illicit uses, such as money laundering and terrorist financing. The legal basis for this role is the Bank Secrecy Act (BSA).[15] FinCEN administers the act by developing and implementing regulations and other guidance and working with private financial institutions and eight federal agencies to ensure that the financial sector complies with the BSA's reporting requirements.

Financial Management Service

The Financial Management Service (FMS) covers salaries and other expenses related to the operations of the FMS, which is responsible for developing and implementing payment policies and procedures for federal agencies, collecting debts owed to those agencies and state

---

[14] P.L. 110-343. For more information see CRS Report R41427, *Troubled Asset Relief Program (TARP): Implementation and Status*, by Baird Webel.

[15] P.L. 91-508.

governments, and providing financial accounting, reporting, and financing services for the federal government and its agents.

Alcohol and Tobacco Tax and Trade Bureau

The Alcohol and Tobacco Tax and Trade Bureau (ATTB) covers salaries and other expenses related to the activities of ATTB, which was established by the Homeland Security Act of 2002.[16] The bureau is responsible for enforcing certain laws regarding the domestic sale and production of alcohol and tobacco products and preventing harm to consumers by ensuring that the products they regulate comply with federal consumer safety laws.

Bureau of the Public Debt

The Bureau of the Public Debt (BPD) covers salaries and other expenses related to the conduct of public debt operations and the promotion of U.S. bonds.

Community Development Financial Institutions Fund

The Community Development Financial Institutions Fund (CDFIF) provides funding for the activities of the CDFIs, which make investments (in the form of loans, grants, and equity acquisitions) in community development financial institutions. These institutions include community development banks, credit unions, and venture capital funds. They in turn provide financing for affordable housing projects, small businesses, and community development projects in eligible areas. The CDFIF also administers the Bank Enterprise Award (BEA) program and the New Markets tax credit. Since its creation in 1994, CDFIF has awarded over $1.7 billion to community development financial institutions, community development entities (CDEs), and depository institutions insured by the Federal Deposit Insurance Corporation through the CDFI Program, the Native American CDFI Assistance Program, and the BEA program. In addition, the Fund has allocated $33 billion in New Markets tax credits to CDEs.

Internal Revenue Service

The Internal Revenue Service (IRS) covers salaries and other expenses related to the activities of the IRS, whose main responsibilities are to administer federal tax laws and collect revenue. Two critical components of IRS operations and programs are the services it offers taxpayers to help them understand and meet their tax obligations and the enforcement tools it uses to improve voluntary taxpayer compliance and punish those who violate the law. Some appropriated funds are used to develop or upgrade business operations and information systems, as part of an ongoing effort to improve the effectiveness and efficiency of taxpayer services and enforcement.

Table 3 shows pre- and post-sequester amounts for FY2013, the President's FY2014 request, and the amounts recommended by the House and Senate Appropriations Committees for FY2013.

---

[16] P.L. 107-296.

Table 3. Department of the Treasury Appropriations, FY2013-FY2014

(in millions of dollars)

Appropriation Account	FY2013 Pre-sequester	FY2013 Post-sequester	FY2014 Request	FY2014 House Committee	FY2014 Senate Committee	FY2014 Enacted
Departmental Offices (Salaries and Expenses)	$308	$292	$312	$182	$302	
Department-wide Systems and Capital Investments	—	0	3	—	3	
Terrorism and Financial Intelligence	—	—	—	105	—	
Office of Inspector General	30	28	31	31	32	
Treasury Inspector General for Tax Administration	151	143	150	155	156	
Special Inspector General for Troubled Asset Relief Program	42	42	35	35	35	
Community Development Financial Institutions Fund	221	209	225	221	230	
Financial Crimes Enforcement Network	111	105	104	111	112	
Financial Management Service	217	206	—	—	—	
Bureau of the Fiscal Service[a]	—	—	360	359	360	
Alcohol and Tobacco Tax and Trade Bureau	100	95	96	96	101	
Bureau of the Public Debt	172	165	—	—	—	
Payment for Losses in Shipment	2	2	2	2	2	
Internal Revenue Service (total)	11,793	11,199	12,861	8,966	12,070	
Taxpayer Services	*2,235*	*2,123*	*2,413*	*1,900*	*2,316*	
Enforcement[b]	*5,289*	*5,022*	*5,421*	*3,866*	*5,343*	
Operations Support Activities[c]	*3,940*	*3,741*	*4,315*	*2,900*	*4,110*	
Business Systems Modernization	*330*	*313*	*301*	*300*	*301*	
Rescissions: Treasury Forfeiture Fund	(-950)	(-950)	(-950)	(-1,219)	(-1,200)	
Total	**$12,196**	**$11,536**	**$13,229**	**$9,044**	**$12,203**	

Sources: H.Rept. 113-172, S.Rept. 113-80, and the Department of the Treasury.

Notes: Figures are rounded and may not sum due to rounding. "Pre-sequester FY2013" figures are from S.Rept. 113-80. "Post-sequester FY2013" amounts provided by the Treasury and reflect the enacted full-year continuing resolution, a sequestration reduction of 5%, and an across-the-board rescission of 0.2% under the Consolidated and Further Continuing Appropriations Act, 2013 (P.L. 113-6).

a. As it did with the FY2013 budget request, Treasury is proposing to merge the appropriation accounts for the Financial Management Service and the Bureau of Public Debt into a single account called the Bureau of Fiscal Service. The main justification for such a consolidation is to improve the efficacy and efficiency of Treasury's financial management operations.

b. The requested appropriation for FY2014 includes $246 million in additional funds as a program integrity cap adjustment for IRS enforcement initiatives to reduce future deficits.

c. The requested appropriation for FY2014 includes $166 million in additional funds as a program integrity cap adjustment for IRS enforcement initiatives to reduce future deficits.

The President's Budget Request

The President requested $13.229 billion (including the cancellation of $950 million in unobligated balances from the Treasury Forfeiture Fund (TFF)) in appropriations for the Department of the Treasury in FY2014. Under the budget proposal, the IRS would receive $12.861 billion, or 97.2% of the total amount. The remaining $1.316 billion (plus $2 million in payments for shipping losses) would be split among Treasury's nine other appropriation accounts in the following amounts: DO, $312 million; Department-wide Systems and Capital Investments Program (DSCIP), $3 million; OIG, $31 million; TIGTA, $150 million; SIGTARP, $35 million; CDFIF, $225 million; FinCEN, $104 million; Fiscal Service Operations (FSO), $360 million (consolidates funding for FMS and BPD); and ATTB, $96 million.

Treasury's FY2014 budget request is intended to promote the following objectives:

- repair and reform the U.S. financial system;

- support recovery in the housing market;

- enhance U.S. competitiveness;

- promote international financial stability and balanced global growth;

- protect national security through targeted financial actions;

- pursue comprehensive tax and fiscal reform; and

- manage the government's finances in a fiscally responsible manner.[17]

More details on the Administration's budget request for each appropriations account follow.

Departmental Offices

The Treasury Department requested $311.8 million in appropriations for DO in FY2014. Of that amount, $36.2 million would go to executive direction, $55.5 million to international affairs and economic policy, $86.1 million to domestic finance and tax policy, $97.7 million to terrorism and

---

[17] For more details on these goals and the ways in which the budget request would promote them, see http://www.treasury.gov/about/budget-performance/CJ14/0.%20Departmential%20Summary.pdf.

financial intelligence, and $36.3 million to Treasury management and related programs.[18] The proposed operating budget would be $381.3 million, which is about $69 million more than the requested appropriations. This difference would be bridged by reimbursable expenses incurred by activities funded under the DO account.

Department-wide Systems and Capital Investments

Treasury requested $2.7 million in appropriations for DSCIP in FY2014. No funds were appropriated for the account in FY2012 and FY2013. Of that amount, $1.5 million would be used to design, procure, and install a "Wireless Intrusion Detection System" in the Main Treasury and Treasury Annex buildings, and $1.2 million would be used to upgrade the energy efficiency of those buildings.[19]

Office of Inspector General

Treasury requested $31.3 million in appropriated funds for OIG in FY2014.[20] The funds would be used to conduct both mandated audits and audits and investigations of Treasury's riskier programs and operations. Among the mandated audits are those related to the Dodd-Frank Wall Street Reform and Consumer Protection Act (Dodd-Frank Act),[21] the Federal Information Security Management Act,[22] the Federal Deposit Insurance Act,[23] and the Improper Payments Elimination and Recovery Act.[24] The OIG is also responsible for conducting audits and investigations of projects and programs funded through the Gulf Coast Restoration Trust Fund and overseeing Treasury's funding of low-income housing projects and certain energy properties under the Economic Recovery and Reinvestment Act of 2009.[25] Included in the budget request was $2.8 million for costs related to OIG's oversight of Gulf Coast Restoration Trust Fund projects and program.

Office of the Special Inspector General for the Troubled Asset Relief Program

Treasury requested $34.9 million for SIGTARP in FY2014.[26] The funds would be used to support the Office's main functions of fostering transparency in Treasury's management of TARP-funded programs for which the federal government has contracts or guarantees; assessing the effectiveness of TARP; and preventing, investigating, and referring for prosecution instances of waste, fraud, and abuse in TARP-funded programs. Included in the budget request were $433,000

---

[18] For more details, see http://www.treasury.gov/about/budget-performance/CJ14/ 1.%20DO%20CJ%20FINAL%20508%20OK.pdf.

[19] For more details, see http://www.treasury.gov/about/budget-performance/CJ14/ 2.%20DSCIP%20CJ%20Final%20508%20OK.pdf.

[20] For more details, see http://www.treasury.gov/about/budget-performance/CJ14/ 3.%20OIG%20CJ%20Final%20ok.pdf.

[21] P.L. 111-203.

[22] 44 U.S.C. §3541, *et seq.*

[23] 12 U.S.C. §1811, *et seq.*

[24] P.L. 112-248.

[25] P.L. 111-5.

[26] For more details, see http://www.treasury.gov/about/budget-performance/CJ14/ 4.%20SIGTARP%20CJ%20Final%20ok.pdf.

for maintaining current levels of operation, $80,000 to support the Council of Inspectors General on Integrity and Efficiency, and $5.8 million in efficiency savings.

Treasury Inspector General for Tax Administration

Treasury requested $149.5 million for TIGTA in FY2014.[27] The appropriated funds would be used to finance the audits, investigations, and evaluations of IRS operations that TIGTA conducts as part of its mission. Among its priorities in FY2014 are reducing the risks associated with IRS's programs for modernizing its business systems, lowering the tax gap, protecting taxpayer identities, and overseeing IRS's efforts to administer the tax provisions of the Patient Protection and Affordable Care Act[28] and the Health Care and Education Reconciliation Act of 2010[29] (henceforth referred to jointly as "ACA"). Included in the budget request were $1.6 million to maintain current operating levels, efficiency savings of $383,000, $5.5 million in program reductions, $324,000 to support the Council of the Inspectors General on Integrity and Efficiency, and $4.5 million to oversee IRS's implementation of the tax provisions in the ACA.

Community Development Financial Institutions Fund

Treasury requested $224.9 million for CDFIF in FY2014.[30] Included in the budget request were $144.3 million for Financial and Technical Assistance awards, $10 million for the BEA program and up to $35 million for the Healthy Food Financing Initiative (HFFI).[31] The request entailed $266,000 to maintain current operating levels, $853,000 in efficiency savings, $11.3 million in program decreases (including an $8 million reduction in funding for the BEA program), and $16.3 million in program increases (including additional funding of $13 million for the HFFI).

Financial Crimes Enforcement Network

Treasury requested $103.9 million for FinCEN in FY2014.[32] Included in the budget request were $1.3 million for maintaining current levels of operation, $2.7 million in efficiency savings, and $6.1 million in program decreases.

Among FinCEN's priorities reported for FY2014 are strengthening relationships with state regulatory agencies to enhance BSA compliance and enforcement, improving enforcement programs by enhancing the identification of illicit financial activities, increasing the number of analytical projects undertaken with foreign financial intelligence units, and refining and applying the new information technology (IT) capabilities made possible by the BSA IT modernization project.

---

[27] For more details, see http://www.treasury.gov/about/budget-performance/CJ14/5.%20TIGTA%20CJ%20FINAL%20ok.pdf.

[28] P.L. 111-148.

[29] P.L. 111-152.

[30] For more details, see http://www.treasury.gov/about/budget-performance/CJ14/6.%20CDFI%20CJ%20FINAL%20ok.pdf.

[31] For more information on HFFI see http://www.cdfifund.gov/what_we_do/FinancingHealthyFoodOptions.asp?programID=13.

[32] For more details, see http://www.treasury.gov/about/budget-performance/CJ14/7.%20FinCEN%20CJ%20FINAL%20ok.pdf.

Alcohol and Tobacco Tax and Trade Bureau

Treasury requested $96.2 million for ATTB in FY2014.[33] Included in the budget request were $1.1 million to maintain current operating levels, $1.7 million in new efficiency savings, and an additional $5.0 million for the alcohol and tobacco enforcement program through what is known as a program integrity cap adjustment.[34]

Bureau of the Fiscal Service

Treasury proposed that the budgets for FMS and BPD be merged into a single appropriation account called the Bureau of the Fiscal Service (FS) beginning in FY2014.[35] (It made the same request for FY2013, but Congress did not adopt it.) Under the proposal, FS would receive $360.2 million in FY2014. Included in the budget request were $4.2 million to maintain current operating levels, $11.9 million in new efficiency savings, $5.6 million in program decreases, $11.7 million in reinvestments, and $5.5 million in program increases.

Among FS's indicated priorities for FY2014 are integrating the accounting and information technology operations of FMS and BPD; implementing a government-wide Treasury Account Symbol system to replace four legacy computer systems; creating a mechanism for managing case files in digital form; continuing to develop the Financial Information Repository and to implement the Payment Information Repository; and transferring the operations of the Office of Financial Innovation to FMS from DO.

Treasury Forfeiture Fund (TFF)

Treasury proposed to cancel permanently $950 million in unobligated balances from the TFF in FY2014.[36] This would come on top of a rescission of $950 million in such balances enacted in FY2013.

The Fund serves as the receipt account for the deposit of non-tax assets seized by the bureaus participating in the TFF. These include the IRS's Criminal Investigation unit, the U.S. Secret Service, the Bureau of Customs and Border Patrol, and the Bureau of Immigration and Customs Enforcement. The Treasury Executive Office for Asset Forfeiture (TEOAF) manages the Fund. Money in the Fund covers the operating expenses of TEOAF and supports the enforcement activities of the participating bureaus related to the National Money Laundering Strategy, the Southwest Border Strategy, and federal efforts to combat terrorist financing.

TEOAF estimated that $593 million will be deposited in the Fund from asset forfeitures and recoveries from previous fiscal years in FY2014, leaving $2.0 billion in budgetary resources, or

---

[33] For more details, see http://www.treasury.gov/about/budget-performance/CJ14/ 8.%20TTB%20CJ%20FY%2014%20FINAL%20ok.pdf.

[34] The cap adjustments have their origin in the Budget Enforcement Act of 1990 (P.L. 101-508). For more details, see CRS Report R41901, *Statutory Budget Controls in Effect Between 1985 and 2002*, by Megan S. Lynch; and CRS Report R41965, *The Budget Control Act of 2011*, by Bill Heniff Jr., Elizabeth Rybicki, and Shannon M. Mahan.

[35] For more details, see http://www.treasury.gov/about/budget-performance/CJ14/9.%20Fiscal%20Service%20CJ%20- %20FINAL.pdf.

[36] For more details, see http://www.treasury.gov/about/budget-performance/CJ14/ 17.%20TEOAF%20CJ%20FINAL%20ok.pdf.

32% less than the amount of budgetary resources in FY2013. After allowing for $716 million in administrative expenses and obligatory costs and the proposed cancellation of $950 million in unobligated balances, the net result at the end of FY2014 would be $370 million in such balances, or 24.8% less than the projected result for FY2013.

Internal Revenue Service

Treasury requested $12.9 billion for the IRS in FY2014.[37] Of this amount, $2.4 billion would be used for taxpayer services, $5.7 billion for enforcement (including $246 million as a program integrity cap adjustment[38]), $4.5 billion for operations support (including $166 million as a program integrity cap adjustment), and $301 million for the Business Systems Modernization (BSM) program.

Included in the budget request were $125.7 million to maintain current operations, $254.9 million in efficiency savings, $1.1 billion in program increases, and $37.5 million in reinvestments. Of the proposed funding for program increases, $177 million is intended to improve taxpayer service; $605 million is intended to implement enacted legislation (especially the ACA), identify and prevent taxpayer identity theft and the issuance of fraudulent tax refunds, and boost compliance by investigating offshore tax evasion, implementing new information reporting requirements, strengthening examination and collection programs, increasing audits, and expanding the tax return preparer program implemented in 2011; $349 million is intended to put in place new IT systems to deliver tax credits and meet rising demand for online and self-assistance services; and $5 million is a transfer from the program integrity cap adjustment for IRS's enforcement account to ATTB for its enforcement programs.

The budget request also proposed amending the Balanced Budget and Emergency Deficit Control Act of 1985[39] in order to raise the discretionary budget caps imposed on funding for the IRS. Under the act, Congress created a mechanism for increasing spending allocations among programs that generate a positive return on investment. These allocations are known as program integrity cap adjustments. Under the Administration's proposal, the adjustments would give the IRS an additional $246 million for tax enforcement initiatives and $166 million for operations support in FY2014.

The IRS's budget request for FY2014 is built around the following priorities:

- improving customer telephone service;
- reducing the federal tax gap;
- upgrading agency IT systems to implement the ACA, develop new online services, and promote increased employee collaboration and productivity; and
- building on the advances in the processing of taxpayer accounts made under a program known as Customer Account Data Engine (CADE) 2.

---

[37] For more details, see http://www.treasury.gov/about/budget-performance/CJ14/ 10.%20IRS%20CJ%20FINAL%20v2.pdf.

[38] For more details, see http://www.treasury.gov/about/budget-performance/CJ14/ 5.%20TIGTA%20CJ%20FINAL%20ok.pdf.

[39] P.L. 99-177.

IRS Oversight Board Assessment of the Budget Request for the IRS

The IRS Oversight Board was established by the IRS Reform and Restructuring Act of 1998[40] to oversee the IRS's performance in administering the tax laws, managing its operations, and accomplishing its strategic goals. Section 7802(d) of the federal tax code requires the Board to assess the annual budget proposal submitted by the IRS to the Treasury Department. A key focus of the Board's assessment is the extent to which the proposal supports the short- and long-term strategic objectives of the agency. The same statutory provision requires the President to submit the Board's budget recommendation to Congress along with the budget request for the IRS.

The Board recommended that the IRS receive $13.074 billion in appropriated funds in FY2014, which would be 1.7% more than the budget request for FY2014.[41] In the Board's view, the recommended funding would arrest a reduction in IRS operating levels since FY2010 which has led to an accelerating decline in the agency's performance, as measured by the amount of enforcement revenue collected, the level of service available through the IRS's toll-free assistance line, taxpayer satisfaction with IRS service, and employee morale.

In its review of the Administration's FY2014 budget request, the Board endorsed the request on the grounds that it seemed "appropriate for the IRS to carry out both its statutory and additional new responsibilities," even though the request is $214 million less than the Board's recommended amount."[42] According to the Board's review, the Administration's proposed budget would make needed investments in improving taxpayer service, enforcement, and agency information systems. More specifically, the Board believed the Administration's requested appropriations for taxpayer services would enable the IRS to upgrade its level of toll-free telephone service and educate taxpayers about the tax provisions in the ACA.[43] It also believed the requested funding for enforcement would allow the IRS to pursue three short-term objectives: (1) accelerate its efforts to combat offshore tax evasion through implementing the provisions of the Foreign Account Tax Compliance Act;[44] (2) improve its capability to prevent the issuance of fraudulent tax refunds tied to identity theft; and (3) increase its audits of high-income taxpayers and corporations.[45]

For the Board, a critical consideration in determining how much funding the IRS should receive is the return on investment the added funds would yield. In its review of the budget request, the Board noted that every dollar invested in taxpayer services, enforcement, operations support, and BSM leads to an average return in revenue collected of four dollars.[46]

House Measure (H.R. 2786)

H.R. 2786 as reported by the House Committee on Appropriations would provide $9.044 billion in appropriations (including $1.219 billion in rescissions) for the Treasury Department in

---

[40] P.L. 105-206.

[41] IRS Oversight Board, *FY2014 IRS Budget Recommendation: Special Report* (Washington: May 2013), p. 3.

[42] IRS Oversight Board, *FY2014 IRS Budget Recommendation: Special Report*, p. 3.

[43] IRS Oversight Board, *FY2014 IRS Budget Recommendation: Special Report*, 10.

[44] P.L. 111-147.

[45] IRS Oversight Board, *FY2014 IRS Budget Recommendation: Special Report*, 11.

[46] IRS Oversight Board, *FY2014 IRS Budget Recommendation: Special Report*, 4.

FY2014.This amount is about 32% less than the budget request. Details on recommended funding for each account and the issues addressed by the committee in its report on the bill follow.

Departmental Offices

The committee recommended that DO receive $182.0 million in appropriated funds in FY2014, or 42% less than the budget request. Much of this difference stems from the committee's decision to create a separate appropriation account for the Office of Terrorism and Financial Intelligence beginning in FY2014. In the Administration's budget request, funding for TFI is included in the DO appropriation account.

In its report on H.R. 2786, the committee directed Treasury to submit an operating plan for the resources it receives for DO in FY2014 no later than 30 days after the enactment of the bill. The plan should cover all offices and bureaus within Treasury and provide details on any planned "program changes and major procurements." In addition, the committee directed Treasury to submit a report on "economic warfare and financial terrorism" no more than 90 days after the enactment of the bill.

Alarmed by what it characterizes as the billions of dollars in improper payments made each year for the Earned Income Tax Credit (EITC), the committee directed the department to work with the IRS to develop more effective ways to monitor and curb such payments. As part of this collaboration, Treasury would be required to submit quarterly reports to the House and Senate Appropriations Committees specifying targets for reducing improper EITC payments and describing the steps being taken to reach them.

The committee also included a provision limiting the fees available for obligation by the Office of Financial Research to the amounts provided in appropriations acts beginning in FY2015.

Office of Terrorism and Financial Intelligence

The committee recommended $105.0 million in appropriations for TFI in FY2014, or $7.3 million more than the amount specified for that purpose within the budget request for DO in FY2014. Funding for TFI was folded into the enacted appropriations for DO in FY2013.

The committee directed TFI to make available to the general public the names of the companies that are failing to comply with current sanctions against Iran and the names of foreign entities doing business with Iran's Revolutionary Guard Corps.

Office of Inspector General

The committee recommended that the OIG receive $31.3 million in appropriations in FY2014, or the same amount as the budget request. The committee also directed OIG to submit a report within 90 days of the enactment of the bill on the "separation of funds and activities" between Treasury offices that receive mandatory funding (e.g., Office of Financial Research and Office of Financial Stability) and the offices whose funding is discretionary and whose work is similar (e.g., the Office of Economic Policy and the Office of Domestic Finance).

Treasury Inspector General for Tax Administration

The committee recommended $155.0 million in appropriations for TIGTA in FY2014, or 3.7% more than the budget request.

In its report on H.R. 2786, the committee expressed support for TIGTA's ongoing investigations into identity theft and tax fraud and TIGTA's commitment to monitor the issue until the IRS "significantly reduces the incidence of tax fraud through identity theft and significantly improves the quality of assistance it provides to victims" of such theft. The committee also directed TIGTA to submit a report no later than 90 days after the bill's enactment assessing the extent to which the revenue that new enforcement initiatives are supposed to yield is actually collected.

Special Inspector General for the Troubled Asset Relief Program

The committee recommended that SIGTARP receive $34.9 million funds for FY2014, or the same as the budget request.

In its report on the bill, the committee acknowledged that initial funding for the program was included in the legislation creating it, but that the mandatory appropriations were limited and decrease over time. To sustain SIGTARP's required oversight of the remaining TARP amounts, discretionary appropriations have had increasingly to fill the gap between the mandatory appropriations and the operating expenses of the program. As TARP winds down in the next few years, the committee "expects" that the requests for discretionary appropriations will also steadily shrink.

In addition, the committee encouraged SIGTARP to continue its oversight of two issues related to TARP: the Making Home Affordable Program and the participation in the Small Business Lending Fund by banks that benefited from TARP loans.

Financial Crimes Enforcement Network

The committee recommended $110.8 million for FinCEN in FY2014, 6.6% less than the budget request. According to the committee's report on H.R. 2786, this funding level is intended to allow FinCEN to continue its multi-year effort to modernize its information systems and to ensure that FinCEN is able to respond to the growing volume of requests for assistance from law enforcement and intelligence agencies made possible by the recently activated BSA IT Modernization system.

The committee also directed the agency to submit a progress report on its reorganization effort no later than 45 days after the enactment of the bill. The report should describe the status of the project as of September 30, 2013, discuss the remaining objectives for FY2014, and assess the extent to which the progress made so far represents an improvement over the previous organization.

Treasury Forfeiture Fund

The committee recommended a rescission of $1.219 billion in unobligated balances in the fund, or 28.3% more than the budget request. Current law allows surpluses in the TFF to be used to enhance forfeiture capabilities, to be held in reserve, or to be rescinded temporarily or permanently.

In its report on the bill, the committee pointed out that the TFF was intended to ensure that adequate resources are available to cover the costs of an "effective asset seizure and forfeiture program." Those costs include expenses related to seizing, evaluating, maintaining, protecting, advertising, forfeiting, and disposing of property. In the committee's view, the Fund should not be used to boost the funds available to participating agencies outside the appropriations process. Relying on the Fund to pay for day-to-day operations or new activities gives participating agencies an incentive to pursue cases involving possible forfeitures with high values, instead of focusing attention on "individuals and organizations that perpetrate the worst crimes against society."

The committee directs TFF to submit a table each month showing the interest earned, the forfeiture revenue collected, unobligated balances, expenses to date, and estimated expenses for the remainder of the fiscal year.

Bureau of the Fiscal Service

The committee recommended $359.5 million for FS in FY2014, or 0.2% less than the budget request. Of this amount, $4.2 million would be available until September 30, 2016, for projects to modernize the agency's information systems. Funding is also included for the USAspending.gov initiative, which was launched in December 2007 to provide the public with free, centralized access to information on federal spending, and the Do Not Pay Business Center, which reviews all federal payments and awards before they are issued to prevent ineligible persons and entities from receiving them.

In its report on H.R. 2786, the committee endorsed the proposed consolidation of FMS and BPD into a single appropriation account to be called FS, beginning in FY2014, citing the future cost savings as an important consideration. The committee also directed FS to issue no later than 60 days after the enactment of the bill separate reports on payments made from the Judgment Fund in FY2012 and in FY2013, and to include in each report all fund payments since 2008, except for those whose disclosure is prohibited by court order or current law. The Judgment Fund, which was established in 1956 and is codified at 31 U.S.C. §1304, is a permanent, indefinite appropriation that is used to pay final money judgments and awards against the federal government that are not covered under another source of funds.[47]

Alcohol and Tobacco Tax and Trade Bureau

The committee recommended that ATTB receive $95.7 million in appropriations in FY2014, or 0.5% less than the budget request.

Community Development Financial Institutions Fund

The committee recommended that CDFIF receive $221.0 million in appropriations in FY2014, or 1.7% less than the budget request. Of that amount, $189 million was designated for financial and

---

[47] For more information on the Judgment Fund, see http://www.fms.treas.gov/judgefund/background.html.

technical assistance grants, $12 million for Native Initiatives, and $20 million for administrative expenses.

In its report on the bill, the committee noted that, though the CDFIF is supposed to serve the development needs of territories and rural communities, there is a "lack" of CDFIs in those areas, particularly in economically distressed communities. The committee wants the CDFIF to extend CDFI programs to those communities.

Internal Revenue Service

The committee recommended that the IRS receive $8.966 billion in appropriations in FY2014, or 30.3% less than the budget request. If enacted, a reduction of that magnitude would exceed the largest percentage decline in IRS appropriations since FY1985: a 4.0% decrease from FY1996 to FY1997. An administrative provision in H.R. 2786 would allow the IRS to transfer up to 5% of its total appropriations (3% in the case of enforcement) from one account to another with the prior approval of the House and Senate Committees on Appropriations.

Funding for the IRS is spread among four accounts: taxpayer services, enforcement, operations support, and business systems modernization. The recommended appropriation for each is examined below.

Taxpayer Services

Of the recommended appropriations for the IRS, $1.9 billion would be used for taxpayer services, or 21.3% less than the budget request. Several taxpayer service grant programs (e.g., Tax Counseling for the Elderly and Volunteer Income Tax Assistance) are funded through this account, but the committee's report on H.R. 2786 mentions no funding levels for them.

The committee expressed concern about the rising instances of income tax fraud stemming from taxpayer identity theft. To combat that theft, the Committee directed the IRS to submit a report by January 31, 2014, providing specified details on the extent of the problem from 2009 to 2013 and assessing the effectiveness of the steps taken by the agency to expedite the resolution of cases involving taxpayers who were the victims of identity theft and to prevent future instances of it.

In addition, the committee expressed its opposition to any planned IRS initiative to develop a pre-filled or simple tax return. The committee opposes such an initiative for two reasons: (1) it would impose costly new administrative burdens on the IRS and employers, and (2) it would create a conflict of interest between the IRS's role as the nation's tax collector and enforcer and the role the agency would assume as a "tax preparer and financial advisor." In the committee's view, the IRS should seek the approval of Congress before embarking on a simple tax return pilot program.

Enforcement

As reported by the committee, H.R. 2786 would provide an appropriation of $3.866 billion for tax law enforcement in FY2014, or 31.8% less than the budget request. Of that amount, at least $60.3 million would be used to support IRS's involvement in the Interagency Crime and Drug Enforcement program. None of the recommended appropriation could be used to implement tax provisions in the ACA, and no funds could be transferred to the IRS from the $1 billion fund established by the ACA and managed by HHS to cover expenses incurred by federal agencies in implementing the act.[48]

The committee directed the IRS to submit a report on enforcement similar to the Taxpayer Assistance Blueprint within 180 days of the enactment of the bill. The report should outline the "safeguards" that are in place to prevent IRS employees from taking "inappropriate enforcement actions." It should also describe how IRS field employees conduct their work and how their supervisors and "IRS headquarters oversee them," incorporate comments from the Taxpayer Advocate and the IRS Oversight Board, and be posted on the IRS's website.

In addition, the committee called for some changes to the final regulations issued by the IRS on interest payments made to non-resident aliens after December 31, 2012. The regulations include a list of countries with which the United States has a tax treaty or information exchange agreement. Every country on the list qualifies for automatic information reporting unless the United States determines that a country should not receive such information because of concerns that it would be misused. To address these concerns in the case of countries with a history of human rights abuses, the committee recommended that the IRS consider the following steps: (1) publishing on its public website a list of countries with which it is actively and automatically exchanging information about interest payments to non-resident aliens living in those places; and (2) creating a program to monitor the compliance of these countries with the requirements for confidentiality and taxpayer safety.

Operations Support

The committee recommended that the IRS receive an appropriation of $2.900 billion for operations support in FY2014, or 35.3% less than the budget request. None of the funds could be used to implement the tax provisions in the ACA.

Business Systems Modernization

As reported by the committee, H.R. 2786 would provide $300.0 million for the BSM program in FY2014, or 0.3% less than the budget request.

The committee commended the IRS for the progress that has been made in the past few years with the Customer Account Data Engine 2 (CADE 2) program, which was launched in January 2012 and used during the 2012 filing season. As a result, records for 140 million individual taxpayer accounts are now stored in a single, modern database, and the records can be updated daily, which makes it possible to issue refunds and communicate with taxpayers about issues with their accounts faster. While the committee recognized that the IRS continues to add capabilities to CADE 2, such as linking historical to current returns, it noted that the "major costs of development and implementation are completed." Thus the committee expects BSM funding requests to start to decline as the "IRS realizes savings from retiring legacy systems."

---

[48] For more information on the fund, see CRS Report R41390, *Discretionary Spending in the Patient Protection and Affordable Care Act (ACA)*, coordinated by C. Stephen Redhead.

Other Issues

As reported by the committee, H.R. 2786 would also impose the following restrictions on the IRS:

- Videos produced by the IRS must be approved in advance by the Service-Wide Video Editorial Board.

- No employee awards or bonuses may be given out until the IRS submits a report to the Committee on "employee salaries and awards and an evaluation of its employee awards program."

- No funds may be used for conferences until the IRS puts in place the key findings from a recent TIGTA audit.

Senate Measure (S. 1371)

S. 1371 as reported by the Senate Committee on Appropriations provided for a total appropriation of $12.203 billion for the Treasury Department in FY2014, including a rescission of $1.2 billion from the TFF. This amount is 7.8% less than the budget request. Details on the funding recommended by the committee for each Treasury account follow. They are based on the committee's report on the bill.

Departmental Offices

The committee recommended that DO receive an appropriation of $302.4 million in FY2014, or 3.0% less than the budget request. An additional $7.4 million would be available for Treasury to administer the RESTORE Act;[49] the funds would come from the trust fund established by the act.

In its report on S. 1371, the committee issued several directives to Treasury related to activities funded under the DO account. One directive instructed the agency to "prioritize" resources for the Office of Terrorism and Financial Intelligence to support its efforts to protect the nation's financial systems against illegal activities such as money laundering. As part of this project, the committee directed Treasury to submit a report within 180 days of the enactment of the bill that assesses the progress made in implementing the recommendations in the 2007 National Money Laundering Strategy; the report should include the views of the Departments of Justice and Homeland Security.

Another directive instructed Treasury to collaborate with the Federal Deposit Insurance Corporation, the Office of the Comptroller of the Currency, the National Credit Union Administration, and the Federal Reserve to offer "clear guidance" to students on the risks associated with private student loans compared to the risks associated with other kinds of debt, and to lenders on the need for flexibility in working with borrowers with private student loan debt to avoid bankruptcy.

The committee also directed the agency to fully implement all sanctions and divestment measures imposed on North Korea, Belarus, Burma, Iran, Sudan, Syria, Zimbabwe, and designated rebel

---

[49] P.L. 112-141.

groups operating in and around the Congo, and to notify the committee if a lack of resources impedes this process. Treasury was also directed to submit a report to several House and Senate committees within 60 days of the enactment of the bill listing the persons in and around the Congo affected by the asset freeze mandated by Section 1284 of the National Defense Authorization Act for Fiscal Year 2013,[50] and to use its resources to combat money laundering related to illegal trade in ivory.

S. 1371 would require Treasury to submit a Capital Investment Plan to the House and Senate Appropriations Committees within 30 days of the release of the President's annual budget request. The plan should include estimates of the funding needed over the lifetime of current and planned capital projects and "meaningful and understandable" summaries of the projects by type. The committee directed Treasury's Office of the Chief Information Officer to determine if adequate resources are being channeled into the projects listed in the plan and the maintenance and modernization of existing systems and to ensure that all projects are "properly tracked and completely described" in the plan.

The committee "encourages" Treasury's Office of Financial Education to assess the effectiveness of current financial literacy programs and develop a set of "measurable" objectives that the Financial Literacy and Education Commission can use to better serve the needs of U.S. adults, particularly given the low rate of financial literacy among this population.

Department-Wide Systems and Capital Investments Programs

The committee recommended $2.7 million in appropriations for DSCIP in FY2014, or the same amount as the budget request. There were no appropriations for the account in FY2013.

Office of Inspector General

The committee recommended $32.0 million in appropriations for OIG in FY2014, or 1.9% more than the budget request. An additional $2.8 million would be available from funds in the trust fund established under the RESTORE Act to enable OIG to conduct required audits and investigations of Treasury's efforts to implement the act.

In its report on S. 1371, the committee directed OIG to perform audits of Treasury's programs to combat money laundering and terrorist financing, its management of capital investments and planning of capital projects, and the CDFIF.

Treasury Inspector General for Tax Administration

The committee recommended that TIGTA receive $156.4 million in appropriated funds for FY2014, or 4.6% more than the budget request. This increase reflects the committee's recognition that TIGTA's workload has been growing in recent years as IRS's operations have expanded and the challenges faced by the IRS have become more complex.

In its report on S. 1371, the committee directed TIGTA to bring to the committee's attention any evidence it uncovers that the IRS is failing to take steps to correct "systemic deficiencies" and to

---

[50] P.L. 112-239.

implement procedures that would prevent the agency from engaging in practices that undermine the public's trust in the IRS's ability to administer the tax laws fairly and efficiently.

The committee also commended TIGTA for its ongoing reviews of IRS's BSM program and other IT projects and noted that it shares the concern expressed by TIGTA in a recent audit report that the IRS is developing and using modernized IT systems without giving adequate thought to their "security implications."

Special Inspector General for the Troubled Asset Relief Program

The committee recommended that SIGTARP receive $34.9 million in appropriations in FY2014, or the same as the budget request. A portion of the recommended decrease from FY2013 levels would be offset by funds carried over from FY2013.

Financial Crimes Enforcement Network

The committee recommended $112.0 million in appropriations for FinCEN in FY2014, or 7.8% more than the budget request. The increase is intended to allow FinCEN to maintain critical functions, "better leverage taxpayer investments in newly enhanced information systems," and reap the benefits from its reorganization during FY2013.

In its report on S. 1371, the committee commended the agency for the progress it has made in modernizing the information system it uses to enforce the Bank Secrecy Act. In the committee's view, the upgrades to FinCEN's system should enhance the capability of Treasury and other government agencies to effectively combat financial crimes.

The committee directed the agency to continue to submit semiannual reports summarizing the progress made in the modernization effort; the reports should emphasize planned goals that were achieved, costs, management of contractors, management of procurement, and strategies for involving all the major stakeholders. In addition, the committee directed FinCEN to improve the reliability and comprehensiveness of BSA data by implementing the recommendations made by the GAO and OIG in recent reports.

FinCEN was also directed to submit to the committee semiannual reports on the status of its reorganization effort. The final report should be submitted one year after the reorganization is complete.

Treasury Forfeiture Fund

The committee recommended a rescission of $1,200 million in unobligated balances in the fund in FY2014, or 26.3% more than the budget request.

Bureau of the Fiscal Service

The committee endorsed a proposal by Treasury to combine FMS and BPD into a single appropriation account called the Bureau of the Fiscal Service (FS), starting in FY2014. FS would receive $360.2 million in appropriated funds for FY2014, or the same as the budget request.

In S. 1371, the committee authorized FS to keep enough of the assets Treasury recovers through its unclaimed asset recovery program to cover the cost of the program. Any remaining assets should be deposited in the General Fund of the Treasury for deficit reduction.

Section 118 of the bill authorized Treasury to transfer funds from the salaries and expenses account for FS to the Debt Collection Fund to cover expenses related to debt collection. Any such transfer would be reimbursed to FS account from debt payments deposited in the Fund.

Alcohol and Tobacco Tax and Trade Bureau

The committee recommended that ATTB receive $100.7 million in appropriations in FY2014, or 4.7% above the budget request. This amount does not include the proposed transfer of funds from the IRS under the program integrity cap adjustment.

In its report on S. 1371, the committee noted that the recommended funding includes $2 million for the cost of hiring special law enforcement agents to combat tobacco smuggling and other criminal activities within the jurisdiction of ATTB.

Community Development Financial Institutions Fund

The committee recommended $230.0 million in appropriations for the CDFIF in FY2014, or 2.3% more than the budget request.

Of this amount, $25.0 million was designated for the Health Food Financing Initiative, which seeks to expand the supply of affordable, wholesome foods in underserved urban and rural communities. The recommended funding is intended to increase financing in these communities for new grocery stores, improved distribution networks for such foods, and the acquisition of the supplies and equipment needed to expand the availability of these foods. The committee also directed CDFIF to encourage recipients of funds to include food hubs in their plans for increasing the supply of affordable, wholesome foods in targeted communities.

In its report on S. 1371, the committee specified that $15 million should be set aside for grants, loans, and technical training and assistance for Native American, Alaskan, and Hawaiian communities.

The bill also would allow Treasury to guarantee up to $1 billion in bonds in FY2014 to support lending and investments by CDFIs in underserved communities. The bond guarantees, authorized under the Small Business Jobs Act of 2010,[51] are be intended to open up new sources of long-term capital. Funds raised through the bonds could be used to back new loans or refinance existing ones. In addition, the recommended appropriations for CDFIF include $2 million to support the fund's continuing efforts to enhance the capacity of CDFIs to support the development of "entrepreneurial" businesses in underserved communities.

---

[51] P.L. 111-240.

Internal Revenue Service

The committee recommended that the IRS receive an appropriation of $12.070 billion in FY2014, or 6.2% less than the budget request. Section 101 of S. 1371 allows the IRS to transfer up to 5% of the amount appropriated for one of its accounts to another account, with one exception: no more than 3% of the amount appropriated for enforcement may be transferred to another account.

In its report on S. 1371, the committee commented on several matters of concern. Specifically, it endorsed the combined use of several recommended approaches to shrinking the tax gap. These include improved information reporting and taxpayer services, increased research into non-compliance, and use of new technology to enhance IRS's enforcement capabilities. The committee also "strongly supports" the research on taxpayer compliance being done by the National Taxpayer Advocate and the IRS Office of Research; directs the IRS to include details on planned reorganizations, job cuts or increases, and changes to current service and enforcement activities in the operating plan the agency is required to submit along with its annual budget request; and instructs the IRS to provide details on the expected hiring dates for staff who will be working on proposed new initiatives, starting with its budget request for FY2015.

Taxpayer Services

The committee recommended that the IRS receive an appropriation of $2.316 billion in FY2014 for taxpayer services, or 4.0% below the budget request.

Of the recommended funding, "not less than" $5.6 million should be used for the Tax Counseling for the Elderly program, at least $10 million should go to low-income taxpayer clinic grants, and at least $18 million should be set aside over two consecutive fiscal years for the Volunteer Income Tax Assistance (VITA) matching grant program. With regard to VITA, the committee "urges" the IRS to permit national organizations involved in coordinating local community efforts to provide tax services for disabled individuals to apply for VITA grants.

In its report on S. 1371, the committee acknowledged what it calls the "important" contribution that IRS's toll-free telephone service makes to taxpayer compliance and noted the recent decline in the level of telephone service. In calendar year 2012, the IRS answered 68% of the calls it received on its toll-free line, and the average wait time for a caller was 17 minutes. Section 104 of the bill specifies that funding will be available in FY2014 for improving the toll-free telephone assistance the IRS offers to taxpayers. Among the committee's recommended improvements are reducing wait times and speeding up correspondence with "victims of tax crimes."

The committee also expressed its approval of the steady rise in the number of taxpayers filing their returns electronically with no additional costs. During the 2012 filing season, 81% of individual returns were e-filed, up from nearly 76% in 2011. E-filing yields substantial cost savings: the IRS estimates that the cost of processing an electronic return is one-twentieth of the cost for a paper return. Considering the rising use of e-filing, IRS's newly acquired ability to process returns on a daily basis, and the growing popularity of the electronic deposit of refunds, the committee "strongly urges" the IRS to update its measure of refund timeliness using the recommendations from the GAO and the IRS Oversight Board.

Deeming it "imperative" that taxpayer service in Alaska and Hawaii remain on a par with the service available in the other 48 states, the committee directed the IRS to ensure that Taxpayer Advocate Service Centers in those states are fully staffed (including a collection technical advisor and an examination technical advisor at each center) and able to resolve even the most complex of taxpayer problems.

Enforcement

The largest Treasury appropriation account covers tax enforcement activities. For FY2014, the committee recommended that the IRS receive $5.343 billion for such activities, or 5.7% less than the budget request (including $246 million from a program integrity cap adjustment for the collection of future revenue). At least $60.3 million of the recommended funds are reserved for the Interagency Crime and Drug Enforcement program.

Citing the findings of a recent report by TIGTA, the committee expressed outrage over the IRS's use of "inappropriate screening criteria" in the processing of applications for tax exempt status by entities claiming to be social welfare organizations under Section 501(c)(4) of the federal tax code.[52] The committee also criticized the agency for problems uncovered by the report that it says contributed to the inappropriate screening, especially "unacceptable delays in case disposition, weak internal controls, communication breakdowns, and serious management deficiencies." To restore the public's trust in the IRS, the committee directed the agency to adopt and adhere to a plan based on the IRS Commissioner's assessment of the screening delays and the steps that need to be taken to ensure they do not recur.[53] Section 109 of the bill requires the IRS to provide clear guidance on its website for the processing of applications for tax-exempt status by social welfare organizations involved in political campaigns, and Section 110 would require the IRS establish managerial controls to ensure that such applications are processed promptly on the basis of "objective criteria."

Noting that identity theft is a growing source of tax fraud, the committee recommended that the IRS invest in new technologies and methods designed to counter such theft. These include unique identifiers to keep potential thieves from gaining access to social security and taxpayer identification numbers and an "identity and linking technology" to facilitate the automatic recognition of duplicate tax returns. The committee directed the IRS to develop and implement and to share with the committee, within 90 days of the enactment of the bill, an "action plan and timetable" for lowering by half the average amount of time a taxpayer victimized by identity theft has to wait to resolve a tax refund fraud claim.

Another issue addressed by the committee was payroll tax fraud. This arises when a payroll tax processor fails to transmit to the IRS the payroll tax revenue it collects from companies that use its services. The committee directed the IRS to increase its scrutiny of payroll processors engaging in "questionable practices" (without specifying any such practices) and to remind all taxpayers using the services of such processors that it is the taxpayer's responsibility to pay all federal and state payroll taxes, regardless of the terms of their contract with the processors. The committee also instructed the agency to submit a report no later than 90 days after the enactment of the bill detailing the data on delinquent payroll processors that are currently collected, how that data are being used to reduce or prevent payroll tax fraud, and what steps the IRS would take if it were given additional resources to combat such fraud. Section 108 of the bill requires the IRS to

---

[52] See http://www.treasury.gov/tigta/auditreports/2013reports/201310053fr.pdf.

[53] See http://www.irs.gov/pub/newsroom/Initial%20Assessment%20and%20Plan%20of%20Action.pdf.

give special consideration to applications for an offer in compromise by taxpayers who are the victim of payroll tax fraud.

Agreeing with a recommendation from the IRS Oversight Board, the committee "strongly urges" the IRS to develop more measures for evaluating the efficacy of several initiatives taken by the agency to improve taxpayer compliance. Four such initiatives were mentioned in the report on S. 1371: tax preparer regulation, the new information reports for merchant payment cards and the basis of stock sold on exchanges, the Compliance Assurance Program, and the Offshore Voluntary Disclosure Program.

Yet another enforcement issue addressed by the committee was the misclassification of workers as independent contractors. Such an error usually leads to the underreporting and underpayment of employment and payroll taxes by employers and workers. To get a better understanding of the extent of the problem, the IRS is undertaking a three-year study of worker classification and other employment tax issues. It has also formed a team to assist taxpayers on tax issues related to the classification of workers. Underscoring its concern about the revenue losses from the misclassification of workers, the committee deemed it "crucial" that the IRS maintain adequate staffing in a program (SS-8) designed to assist employers in determining a worker's employment tax status. The committee directed the agency, before reducing staffing at any SS-8 processing office, to submit a report that examines staffing levels, employee productivity, and SS-8 receipts over the past five years and clearly explains the rationale for the proposed reduction.

On the matter of collecting delinquent individual tax debt, Section 105 of the bill would extend through FY2014 a ban on using appropriated funds to "enter into, renew, extend, administer, implement, enforce, provide oversight of, or make any payment related to" a debt collection program involving the use of private debt collectors. The ban, which was first imposed on FY2010 appropriations as a result of Consolidated Appropriations Act, 2010,[54] is intended to reinforce a decision by the IRS in March 2009 to terminate a controversial private tax debt collection program that had begun three years earlier.[55]

Operations Support

For FY2014, the committee recommended that the IRS receive $4.110 billion in appropriations for operations support, or 8.3% less than the budget request. Up to $250 million of the recommended funds would be available for IT support through the end of FY2015; another $1 million would be available for research through the end of FY2016; and at least $2 million would go to the IRS Oversight Board to pay for its operating expenses.

In its report on S. 1371, the committee noted that the IRS lacks a "comprehensive integrated system" for evaluating the agency's performance, productivity, and program costs. This deficiency includes the lack of a quantitative measure of the progress made in implementing major non-BSM IT projects. To remedy these gaps in IRS's management of its IT projects, the committee "strongly urges" the agency to consider developing such a measure, which would give IRS managers and congressional staff a better understanding of the results of its investments in major new IT projects.

---

[54] P.L. 111-117.

[55] For more details, see David Lawder, "U.S. IRS to end contracts with private tax debt collectors," *Reuters*, March 5, 2009, available at http://www.reuters.com/article/2009/03/06/usa-taxes-idUSN0536345520090306.

The committee also directed the IRS to submit within 180 days of the enactment of the bill a strategic plan for new uses of its e-services and the resources needed to implement them.

In addition, the IRS was directed to include in its budget request for FY2015 a long-term strategy for upgrading its aging legacy computer systems The agency must also submit to the House and Senate Appropriations Committees and GAO quarterly reports in FY2014 that discuss in plain English the costs and schedules for the previous three months and the anticipated costs and schedules for the next three months for several IT projects, including IRS.gov, Returns Remittance Processing, EDAS/IPM, Information Returns and Documents Processing, and E-services.

Business Systems Modernization

IRS maintains a separate appropriation account for the BSM program. The committee recommended that the program receive $300.8 million in appropriations in FY2014, or the same as the budget request. To augment funding for BSM in FY2014, the committee encouraged the agency to draw upon user fees collected by the IRS.

In its report on S. 1371, the committee recognized that "sustained and adequate funding" is critical to the success of risky IT modernization projects like the BSM program and notes that it is committed to enabling the IRS to build on the progress it made in 2012 with the CADE 2 and Modernized e-File (MeF) programs.

The committee "expects" the IRS to continue to submit quarterly BSM reports to the Committee and the GAO during FY2014. The reports should clearly explain the costs and schedules for CADE 2 and MeF in the previous three months and their anticipated costs in the next three months.

Executive Office of the President[56]

The FSGG appropriations bill provides funding for all but three offices under the EOP.[57] The White House, the Office of Management and Budget, and the Office of National Drug Control Policy are among the EOP offices funded through FSGG appropriations. **Table 4** lists the amounts for FY2013 prior to the sequester, the President's FY2014 request, and amounts recommended by the House and Senate appropriations committees for FY2014.

---

[56] This section authored by Barbara Schwemle (x7-8655).

[57] Of the three exceptions, the Council on Environmental Quality and the Office of Environmental Quality are funded in the House and Senate Interior, Environment, and Related Agencies Appropriations Act. The Office of Science and Technology Policy and the Office of the United States Trade Representative are funded in the House and Senate Commerce, Justice, Science, and Related Agencies Appropriations Act.

Table 4. Executive Office of the President Appropriations, FY2013-FY2014

(in millions of dollars)

	FY2013 Pre-Sequester	FY2014 Request	FY2014 House Committee	FY2014 Senate Committee	FY2014 Enacted
The White House (total)	$201	$199	$175	$199	
Compensation of the President	*0.5*	*0.5*	*0.5*	*0.5*	
The White House Office (salaries and expenses)	*57*	*55*	*50*	*55*	
Executive Residence, White House (operating expenses)	*13*	*13*	*12*	*13*	
White House Repair and Restoration	*0.8*	*0.8*	*0.8*	*0.8*	
Council of Economic Advisers	*4*	*4*	*4*	*4*	
National Security Council and Homeland Security Council	*13*	*13*	*10*	*13*	
Office of Administration	*113*	*113*	*98*	*113*	
Office of Management and Budget	89	93	79	93	
Federal Drug Control Programs (total)	368	311	361	367	
Office of National Drug Control Policy (net of rescissions)	*24*	*23*	*22*	*23*	
High Intensity Drug Trafficking Areas Program	*238*	*193*	*238*	*238*	
Other Federal Drug Control Programs	*106*	*95*	*100*	*106*	
Unanticipated Needs	1	1	0	1	
Information Technology Oversight and Reform	5	0	5	8	
Data-driven Innovation	0	14	0	6	
Special Assistance to the President (salaries and expenses)	4	4	4	4	
Official Residence of the Vice President (operating expenses)	0.3	0.3	0.3	0.3	
Total: EOP and Funds Appropriated to the President	**$669**	**$623**	**$625**	**$679**	

Sources: H.Rept. 113-172 and S.Rept. 113-80.

Notes: All figures are rounded, and columns may not equal the total due to rounding. "Pre-sequester FY2013" figures are from S.Rept. 113-80 and include across-the-board cuts under the Consolidated and Further Continuing Appropriations Act, 2013 (P.L. 113-6). The Information Technology Oversight and Reform account is labeled as Integrated, Efficient and Effective Uses of Information Technology in S. 1371.

The President's Budget Request and Key Issues

The Administration's FY2014 budget requested an appropriation (discretionary funds) of $623.5 million for the EOP and funds appropriated to the President.

The justification that accompanied the EOP's budget submission noted that the increase requested for the Office of Administration would, among other items, fund salaries and benefits resulting from "the conversion of ten contractors to full-time Government staff," the monthly transit subsidy, and equipment.[58]

According to the justification, the requested increase for the Office of Management and Budget would allow the agency to maintain a staffing level of 506 FTE in FY2014 (+$3.3 million), fund anticipated cost increases in GSA rental payments (+$174,000) and information technology contractor support (+$363,000), and allow the agency to implement a Senior Executive Service Candidate Development Program (+$550,000).[59] In addition, according to the justification, the reductions in requested appropriations resulted from "the Administration's commitment to identify and demonstrate real spending reductions."

The President's budget request proposed an administrative provision for the EOP and funds appropriated to the President at Section 201 that would continue to authorize the OMB Director (or other official designated by the President) to transfer up to 10% of appropriations between the White House, Executive Residence at the White House, White House Repair and Restoration, Council of Economic Advisers, National Security Council and Homeland Security Council, Office of Administration, Special Assistance to the President, and Official Residence of the Vice President accounts, provided the House and Senate Committees on Appropriations are notified at least 15 days in advance. An appropriation could not be increased by more than 50% by such transfers. The Vice President would approve transfers from the Special Assistance to the President or Official Residence of the Vice President accounts.[60]

Federal Drug Control Programs

For the accounts under the Federal Drug Control Programs account, the President's FY2014 budget requested a total appropriation of $311.4 million.

The FY2014 budget justification stated that the ONDCP funding would enable the agency "to continue to pursue" the National Drug Control Strategy's "goals of reducing drug use and its consequences and ensuring improvements in fostering healthier individuals and safe communities by sustaining and building upon significant accomplishments." The requested reduction in the High Intensity Drug Trafficking Areas Program (HIDTAP) appropriation would occur in the grants to state, local, and tribal agencies, and transfers to federal agencies participating in the 28 High Intensity Drug Trafficking Areas. The Other Federal Drug Control Programs appropriation

---

[58] U.S. Executive Office of the President, *Fiscal Year 2014 Congressional Budget Submission* (Washington: April 2013), p. OA-4.

[59] U.S. Executive Office of the President, *Fiscal Year 2014 Congressional Budget Submission*, p. OMB-5.

[60] *Appendix, Budget of the United States, FY2014*, p. 1127.

would be allocated to the Drug Free Communities Program ($85.7 million), anti-doping activities ($7.8 million), and World Anti-Doping Agency membership dues ($1.9 million).[61]

House Measure (H.R. 2786)

H.R. 2786 as reported by the House Committee on Appropriations would provide an appropriation of $624.4 million for the EOP, which is $927,000 (+0.15%) more than the President's request for FY2014. The House report stated the committee's belief "that the chief executive of any organization experiencing a fiscal crisis should share in the funding sacrifice along with the rest of the organization" and noted that the FY2014 appropriations for the White House, the Executive Residence, the Council of Economic Advisors, the National Security and Homeland Security Councils, the Office of Administration, the Office of Management and Budget, the Special Assistant to the President, and the Official Residence of the Vice President were 15% less than the FY2010 level.[62]

The appropriations for each of the EOP accounts, as recommended by the House Appropriations Committee, were as follows:

- The White House Office: $50.3 million; $4.8 million (-8.8%) less than the President's request. The House committee report stated that this amount includes "sufficient funds" for the Office of National AIDS Policy.

- Executive Residence, White House: $11.8 million; $1 million (-7.9%) less than the President's request.

- White House Repair and Restoration: $750,000; the same as the President's request.

- Council of Economic Advisers: $3.6 million; $622,000 (-14.8%) less than the President's request.

- National Security Council and Homeland Security Council: $10.4 million; $2.2 million (-17.6%) less than the President's request.

- Office of Administration: $98 million; $15.1 million (-13.4%) less than the President's request. Of the total, up to $12 million would remain available until expended for continued modernization of the information technology infrastructure within the EOP. The office is directed to report annually to the House Committee on Appropriations, at the same time that the President's budget is submitted, on progress on modernization of information technology, including the amounts obligated and expended and for what purposes, specific milestones achieved, and requirements and specific plans for further investment.

- Office of Management and Budget: $79 million; $14.5 million (-15.5%) less than the President's request.

---

[61] U.S. Executive Office of the President, Fiscal Year 2014 *Congressional Budget Submission Executive Office of the President Office of National Drug Control Policy* (Washington: April 2013), pp. 12, 46, 31, and 36-37.

[62] H.Rept. 113-172, pp. 23-24.

The House committee report included guidance and directives for OMB, as follows.[63]

The report stated that the committee "provides sufficient funds for OMB to consult with and provide Congressional committees with an appropriate number of printed and electronic copies" of the FY2015 budget, including the Appendix, Historical Tables and Analytical Perspectives volumes. The committee report indicated that "in non-transition years, the Administration should be held to the statutory deadline for submission of the budget request" and limited the level of funding available to OMB until the budget request is submitted.

Stating that OMB "should work toward presenting its budget request and financial plans in a manner that allocates all OMB obligations by office or activity," the agency was directed to provide the House and Senate Appropriations Committees with quarterly reports on obligations by object class and full-time equivalents (FTE) by office. The reports are to display actual and estimated obligations and FTE, to date and for the remainder of the fiscal year, and contain obligation information regarding the operations of the core budgeting system.

The report stated the committee's expectation that OMB would ensure the long term effectiveness of the Office of the Intellectual Property Enforcement Coordinator (IPEC) by hiring permanent senior staff and directs the agency to report to the committee within 120 days of the act's enactment on the IPEC budget, including the number of permanent FTEs.

According to the report, the committee was "concerned that Federal agencies purchasing online advertisements may unwittingly have advertisements appear on websites operated by those engaged in criminal activity, including sites proliferating malware, or engaged in identity theft, theft of intellectual property or counterfeiting." The committee believed that OMB should review the issue and provide any necessary guidance to executive branch agencies, and directed the agency to report to the committee on its progress within 180 days of the act's enactment.

OMB was directed to report to the committee, within 120 days after the act's enactment, on agency compliance with OMB Memorandum M-12-12 on reducing travel expenses and conference spending. The report is to identify each agency's savings, whether the 30% savings goal was achieved, the impact of changes in travel and conference policies on the ability of agencies to perform mission critical activities, and recommendations to improve OMB's policies on travel.

The report stated that the committee believed that OMB should "provide guidance to agencies on transaction-based and no-cost funding models, including when it is appropriate to consider using these contract tools, how to calculate potential savings from their use, and standards and best practices for conducting their procurement." OMB was directed to report within 90 days after the act's enactment on the use of such models for procuring information technology goods and services. The report is to include "information on (a) transaction-based or no-cost funding model use by agencies; (b) quantifiable costs savings and cost avoidance through their use; (c) plans to continue or expand their future use; and (d) the status of the issuance of guidance to agencies regarding their use."

---

[63] H.Rept. 113-172., pp. 26-28.

The committee encouraged OMB and federal agencies to use successful business management techniques, including continuous process improvement methods, to assist in meeting performance goals and reducing wasteful spending.

- Unanticipated Needs: No funding for FY2014; $1 million (-100%) less than the President's request.

- Information Technology Oversight and Reform: $5.0 million;[64] the OMB Director could transfer the funds to one or more agencies to carry out projects and would submit quarterly reports, not later than 30 days after the end of each quarter, to the House and Senate Committees on Appropriations identifying the savings achieved by the government-wide information technology reform efforts by fiscal year, agency, and appropriation.

- Special Assistance to the President: $3.9 million; $415,000 (-9.6%) less than the President's request.

- Official Residence of the Vice President: $281,000; $26,000 (-8.5%) less than the President's request.

H.R. 2786 as reported would fund the federal drug control accounts at the following levels:

- ONDCP: $22.5 million; $147,000 (-0.6%) less than the President's request. The agency was expected "to focus resources on the counter-drug policy development, coordination and evaluation functions which are the primary mission of the Office and the original reason for its existence."

- HIDTAP: $238.5 million; $45.1 million (+23.3%) more than the President's request. Not less than 51% of the funds would be transferred to state and local entities for drug control activities and would be obligated within 120 days after the act's enactment. Up to 49% of the funds could be transferred to federal agencies and departments as determined by the ONDCP Director, of which up to $2.7 million could be used for auditing services and associated activities (including up to $500,000 for the continued operation and maintenance of the Performance Management System). The ONDCP Director would notify the House and Senate Committees on Appropriations of the initial allocation of FY2014 funding among HIDTAs within 45 days after the act's enactment and of planned uses of discretionary HIDTA funding, determined in consultation with the HIDTA Directors, within 90 days after the act's enactment.

- OFDCP: $100.5 million; $5.1 million (+5.4%) more than the President's request. The appropriation would be allocated as follows: $88 million for the Drug-Free Communities Program, $1.1 million for drug court training and technical assistance, $8.5 million for anti-doping activities, $1.9 million for U.S. membership dues to the World Anti-Doping Agency, and $1.0 million for competitive discretionary grants to states to assist in implementing effective drug laws.

---

[64] The President's budget requested an appropriation of $14 million for similar activities under the heading Data-driven Innovation.

Section 626(a)(1) of H.R. 2786 as reported would provide the mandatory appropriation for the compensation of the President ($450,000, including $50,000 for expenses). According to the House Committee on Appropriations report, this is an account "where authorizing language requires the payment of funds."[65]

The House bill as reported included the following EOP administrative provisions:

- Section 201 would continue to authorize the OMB Director (or other official designated by the President) to transfer up to 10% of appropriations between the White House, Executive Residence at the White House, White House Repair and Restoration, Council of Economic Advisers, National Security Council and Homeland Security Council, Office of Administration, Special Assistance to the President, and Official Residence of the Vice President accounts, provided the House and Senate Committees on Appropriations are notified at least 15 days in advance. An appropriation could not be increased by more than 50% by such transfers. The Vice President would approve transfers from the Special Assistance to the President or Official Residence of the Vice President accounts.

- Section 202 would require the OMB Director to report to the House and Senate Committees on Appropriations, within 90 days after the act's enactment, on the costs of implementing the Dodd-Frank Act. The report would include the estimated mandatory and discretionary obligations of funds through FY2018, by federal agency and by fiscal year, including (1) the estimated obligations by cost inputs such as rent, information technology, contracts, and personnel; the methodology and data sources used to calculate such estimated obligations; and the specific section of such act that requires the obligation of funds; and (2) the estimated receipts through FY2018 from assessments, user fees, and other fees by the federal agency making the collections, by fiscal year, including the methodology and data sources used to calculate such estimated collections; and the specific section of such act that authorizes the collection of funds.

- Section 203 would prohibit the use of funds to pay the salaries and expenses of any EOP officer or employee to prepare, sign, or approve statements abrogating legislation passed by the House of Representatives and the Senate and signed by the President.

- Section 204 would prohibit the use of funds to pay the salaries and expenses of any EOP officer or employee to prepare or implement an executive order that contravenes existing law.

- Section 622 of H.R. 2786 as reported would continue the provision prohibiting the use of funds to pay the salaries and expenses for the Director of the White House Office of Health Reform, the Assistant to the President for Energy and Climate Change, the Senior Advisor to the Secretary of the Treasury assigned to the Presidential Task Force on the Auto Industry and Senior Counselor for Manufacturing Policy, and the White House Director of Urban Affairs, or any substantially similar positions.

---

[65] H.Rept. 113-172, p. 121.

The House committee continued the provision at Section 610 that would prohibit the EOP from using funds to request an FBI official background investigation report on any individual except with the express written consent of the individual involved, within six months prior to the date of such request and during the same presidential administration, or when required because of extraordinary circumstances involving national security.

Senate Measure (S. 1371)

S. 1371 as reported by the Senate Committee on Appropriations would provide an appropriation of $679.1 million for the EOP, $55.6 million (+8.9%) more than the President's request.

The appropriations for each of the EOP accounts, as recommended by the Senate Appropriations Committee, were as follows:

- The White House Office: $55.1 million; the same as the President's request. The Senate committee report directed the EOP "to allocate sufficient resources to continue the robust operation of the Office of National AIDS Policy" and "the administration to continue to coordinate a Government-wide effort to continue to coordinate a government-wide effort to achieve the goals of the National HIV/AIDS strategy."[66]

- Executive Residence, White House: $12.8 million; the same as the President's request.

- White House Repair and Restoration: $750,000; the same as the President's request.

- Council of Economic Advisers: almost $4.2 million; the same as the President's request.

- National Security Council and Homeland Security Council: $12.6 million; the same as the President's request.

- Office of Administration: $113.1 million; the same as the President's request. Of the total, $12 million would remain available until expended for continued modernization of the information technology infrastructure within the EOP. According to the Senate report, the continuation of this initiative "will refresh the aging information technology infrastructure, strengthen disaster recovery and information security capabilities, and transition the EOP's communications architecture to integrate mobile devices while complying with security and records management requirements." The office is directed "to place a top priority on the implementation of comprehensive policies and procedures for the preservation of all records, including electronic records such as emails, videos, and social networking communication, consistent with" laws, including the Presidential Records Act and the Federal Records Act. The office is to work closely with the National Archives and Records Administration, and fully apprise the committee of funding needed to preserve and retain records.[67]

---

[66] S.Rept. 113-80, p. 39.

[67] S.Rept. 113-80, p. 41.

- Office of Management and Budget: $93.4 million; the same as the President's request.

The Senate committee report included guidance and directives for OMB, as follows.[68]

OMB was directed to "allocate increased funds toward restoring non-politically appointed civil service staffing levels, including for the Office of Federal Procurement Policy and the Office of Information and Regulatory Affairs," and to use the additional resources to respond to requests from Congress "in a timely and complete manner" and, particularly, those "related to program funding and operations."

As in the House committee report, the Senate report stated that the committee believed that OMB should "provide guidance to agencies on transaction-based and no-cost funding models, including when it is appropriate to consider using these contract tools, how to calculate potential savings from their use, and standards and best practices for conducting their procurement." OMB was directed to report within 90 days after the act's enactment on the use of such models for procuring information technology goods and services. The report is to include "information on (a) transaction-based or no-cost funding model use by agencies; (b) quantifiable costs savings and cost avoidance through their use; (c) plans to continue or expand their future use; and (d) the status of the issuance of guidance to agencies regarding their use."

The committee directed OMB to continue making enhancements to the federal government's core budgeting system, within current resources, and to notify the committee of any cost-effective opportunities for further improvements.

In conjunction with the work of the Chemical Government Coordinating Council and the Chemical Sector Coordination Council, OMB was directed to conduct a comprehensive review of the regulatory regime related to chemical security and then report the findings to the committee within 180 days after the act's enactment. The report is to (1) identify regulatory gaps that may pose an unacceptable security risk, (2) evaluate the effectiveness of strategies for closing such gaps, (3) identify existing redundancies between current regulatory regimes, and (4) evaluate strategies for eliminating such redundancies. In addition, the report is to describe the coordination by federal entities with responsibilities for chemical security and how coordination can be improved, including through formal agreements.

OMB was directed "to coordinate with the Recovery Accountability and Transparency Board to publish information on its Web site" on the status of funding provided under P.L. 113-2, "including commitments, obligations, unobligated balances, and expenditures" within 60 days after the Hurricane Sandy Rebuilding Task Force terminates, and, thereafter, in quarterly updates.

The agency was directed to submit a report within 90 days after the act's enactment "on the feasibility of producing an analysis of current levels of spending on children and children's programs, including a detailed breakdown by agency, department, and initiative."

The committee report noted that, although OMB required agencies to submit the first draft of their strategic plans, as required by the Government Performance and Results Modernization Act (GPRMA), by June 3, 2013, few of the required agency consultations with the committee staff

---

[68] S.Rept. 113-80, pp. 42-43.

had taken place. Agency representatives were directed to "promptly contact" the staff to schedule the consultations and OMB was requested to facilitate the discussions as necessary.

- Unanticipated Needs: $1.0 million; the same as the President's request.

- Integrated, Efficient and Effective Uses of Information Technology[69]: $8.0 million. The Senate report reminded the Administration to regularly apprise the committee "of how Government-wide IT reform efforts affect agency-specific projects and missions on a case-by-case basis," and to immediately notify the committee of changes in agency spending plans for IT projects. The report directed that "IT reform initiatives shall not be a substitute for the Committee's routine consideration of agency needs" under the budget process.[70]

- Data-driven Innovation: $6 million; $8 million (-57.1%) less than the President's request for this new initiative. The Senate report stated that the committee did not adopt the President's proposal to fund the information technology management program under the Data-driven Innovation account and instead recommended funding for that program under the Integrated, Efficient and Effective Uses of Information Technology account. The committee expected to be regularly apprised of how efforts under the program affect agency- and program-specific projects and missions, on a case-by-case basis and expected the EOP to demonstrate how all changes comply with current law and to notify the committee and relevant authorizing committees on any projects or reforms that will affect program designs, operations, and outcomes. The program was not to be a substitute for the committee's consideration of agency needs or evaluation of program operations under the regular budget and oversight process. The EOP was directed to immediately notify the committee of any change in an agency spending plan resulting from the program.

- Special Assistance to the President: $4.3 million; the same as the President's request.

- Official Residence of the Vice President: $307,000; the same as the President's request.

S. 1371 as reported would fund the federal drug control accounts at the following levels:

- ONDCP: $23.0 million; $353,000 (+1.6%) more than the President's request. Policy research was not funded.

- HIDTAP: $238.5 million; $45.1 million (+23.3%) more than the President's request. The office was directed to provide funding for the existing HIDTAs at not less than the FY2013 level and to consult with the HIDTAs prior to allocating funds. Of the total, up to $2.7 million could be used for auditing services and associated activities. HIDTA funds are to be expeditiously transferred to the appropriate drug control agencies and are to be withheld from a state "until such time as a State or locality has met its financial obligation."[71]

---

[69] H.R. 2786 as reported labels this account as Information Technology Oversight and Reform.

[70] S.Rept. 113-80, p. 48.

[71] S.Rept. 113-80, p. 45.

- OFDCP: $105.6 million; $10.2 million (+10.7%) more than the President's request. The appropriation would be allocated as follows: $92.0 million for the Drug-Free Communities Support Program (DFCSP), including $2.0 million for National Community Anti-Drug Coalition training; $9.0 million for anti-doping activities; $1.9 million for the United States membership dues to the World Anti-Doping Agency; $1.2 million for activities related to model State drug laws; and $1.4 million for drug court training and technical assistance.

Administrative provisions under the appropriation for the EOP and funds appropriated to the President included in S. 1371 as reported were the following:

- Section 201 would continue to authorize the OMB Director (or other official designated by the President) to transfer up to 10% of appropriations between the White House, Executive Residence at the White House, White House Repair and Restoration, Council of Economic Advisers, National Security Council and Homeland Security Council, Office of Administration, Special Assistance to the President, and Official Residence of the Vice President accounts, after the House and Senate Committees on Appropriations are notified at least 15 days in advance. An appropriation could not be increased by more than 50% by such transfers. The Vice President would approve transfers from the Special Assistance to the President or Official Residence of the Vice President accounts.

- Section 202 would require the ONDCP Director to submit to the Senate and House Appropriations Committees, within 60 days after the act's enactment, and prior to initially obligating more than 20% of the ONDCP funds, "a detailed narrative and financial plan on the proposed uses of all funds under the account by program, project, and activity." The reports must be updated every six months and include any changes in the estimates and assumptions of the previous reports. New projects and changes in the funding for ongoing projects would require advance approval by the committees.

- Section 203 would provide that up to 2% of ONDCP appropriations could be transferred between appropriated programs within ONDCP with advance approval by the Senate and House Committees on Appropriations, but such transfer could not increase or decrease an appropriation by more than 3%.

- Section 204 would provide that up to $1.0 million of ONDCP appropriations could be reprogrammed within a program, project, or activity with advance approval by the Senate and House Appropriations committees.

The Senate committee continued the provision at Section 610 that would prohibit the EOP from using funds to request an FBI official background investigation report on any individual except with the express written consent of the individual involved, within six months prior to the date of such request and during the same presidential administration, or when required because of extraordinary circumstances involving national security.

The Judiciary[72]

As a co-equal branch of government, the judiciary presents its budget to the President, who transmits it to Congress unaltered. The FY2014 judiciary budget request totaled $7.22 billion. **Table 5** lists the pre-sequester amounts for FY2013, the President's FY2014 request, and amounts recommended by the House and Senate appropriations committees for FY2014.

Table 5. The Judiciary Appropriations, FY2013-FY2014

(in millions of dollars)

	FY2013 Pre-sequester	FY2014 Request	FY2014 House Committee	FY2014 Senate Committee	FY2014 Enacted
Supreme Court (total)	$83	$86.5	$86	$86	
Salaries and Expenses	*75*	*74.8*	*74*	*75*	
Building and Grounds	*8*	*11.6*	*12*	*11*	
U.S. Court of Appeals for the Federal Circuit	32	33.4	31	33	
U.S. Court of International Trade	21	22.0	20	21	
Courts of Appeals, District Courts, and Other Judicial Services (total)	6,609	6,822.9	6,644	6,768	
Salaries and Expenses	*5,016*	*5,170.2*	*4,999*	*5,089*	
Defender Services	*1,038*	*1,068.6*	*1,065*	*1,098*	
Fees of Jurors and Commissioners	*52*	*54.4*	*54*	*55*	
Court Security	*499*	*524.3*	*520*	*520*	
Vaccine Injury Trust Fund	*5*	*5.3*	*5*	*5*	
Administrative Office of the U.S. Courts	83	85.4	80	84	
Federal Judicial Center	27	27.7	26	26	
United States Sentencing Commission	16	17.0	16	17	
Judicial Retirement Funds	125	127	127	127	
Total: The Judiciary	**$6,998**	**$7,221.7**	**$7,029**	**$7,161**	

Sources: H.Rept. 113-172 and S.Rept. 113-80.

Notes: All figures are rounded, and columns may not equal the total due to rounding. "Pre-sequester FY2013" figures are from S.Rept. 113-80 and include across-the-board cuts under the Consolidated and Further Continuing Appropriations Act, 2013 (P.L. 113-6).

---

[72] This section authored by Matthew Glassman (x7-3467).

The Judiciary Budget and Key Issues

Appropriations for the judiciary comprise approximately (0.2%) of total budget authority.[73]

Two accounts that fund the Supreme Court (the salaries and expenses of the Court and the expenditures for the care of its building and grounds, which are the responsibility of the Architect of the Capitol) together total approximately 1% of the total judiciary budget. The rest of the judiciary's budget provides funding for the "lower" federal courts and related judicial services.

The largest account, approximately 72% of the total FY2014 budget request—the Salaries and Expenses account for the U.S. Courts of Appeals, District Courts, and Other Judicial Services— covers the "salaries of circuit and district judges (including judges of the territorial courts of the United States), justices and judges retired from office or from regular active service, judges of the U.S. Court of Federal Claims, bankruptcy judges, magistrate judges, and all other officers and employees of the federal judiciary not otherwise specifically provided for," and "necessary expenses of the courts." Two other large accounts provide funds for Defender Services (14.8%) and Court Security (7.3%).

The remaining judiciary budget is divided among the: U.S. Court of Appeals for the Federal Circuit (0.5% in FY2014 request), U.S. Court of International Trade (0.3%), Fees of Jurors and Commissioners (0.8%), Administrative Office of the U.S. Courts (1.2%), Federal Judicial Center (0.4%), U.S. Sentencing Commission (0.2%), and Judicial Retirement Funds (1.8%).

The judiciary budget does not fund three "special courts" in the U.S. court system: the U.S. Court of Appeals for the Armed Forces (funded in the Department of Defense appropriations bill), the U.S. Court of Appeals for Veterans Claims (funded in the Military Construction, Veterans Affairs, and Related Agencies appropriations bill), and the U.S. Tax Court (funded under Independent Agencies, Title V, of the FSGG bill). Federal courthouse construction is funded within the General Services account under Independent Agencies, Title V, of the FSGG bill.

The judiciary uses non-appropriated funds to offset its appropriations requirement. The majority of these non-appropriated funds are from fee collections, primarily from court filing fees. These monies are used to offset expenses within the Salaries and Expenses account of Courts of Appeals, District Courts, and Other Judicial Services. Some of these funds may be carried forward from one year to the next. These funds are considered "unencumbered" because they result from savings from the judiciary's financial plan in areas where budgeted costs did not materialize. According to the judiciary, such savings are usually not under its control (e.g., the judiciary has no control over the confirmation rate of Article III judges and must make its best estimate on the needed funds to budget for judgeships, rent costs based on delivery dates, and technology funding for certain programs).

The judiciary also has "encumbered" funds—no-year authority funds appropriated for specific purposes. These are used when planned expenses are delayed, from one year to the next (e.g., costs associated with space delivery, and certain technology needs and projects).

---

[73] Calculations by CRS with data from *Historical Tables, Budget of the United States Government, FY2014*, Table 5.2—Budget Authority By Agency: 1976–2018; available at http://www.whitehouse.gov/omb/budget/Historicals.

At a March 20, 2013, House hearing, Judge Julia S. Gibbons, chair of the Budget Committee of the Judicial Conference of the United States,[74] addressed funding constraints and efforts to cut costs.[75] She also discussed the potential impact of a sequester pursuant to the Budget Control Act, workload projections, and staffing formulas. She stated that the courts have already downsized by nearly 1,800 employees since July 2011 and that "cuts below the 2012 level—even cuts less severe than sequestration ... [would] result in forced downsizings, delays in processing cases, and a reduction in the supervision of felons on post-conviction release in the community."[76]

Judicial Security[77]

The safe conduct of court proceedings and the security of judges in courtrooms and off-site has been a concern in recent years. The Chicago murders of family members of a federal judge, and the Atlanta killings of a state judge, a court reporter, and a sheriff's deputy at a courthouse in 2005; the sniper shooting of a state judge in his Reno office in 2006; and the wounding of a deputy U.S. marshal and killing of a court security officer at the Lloyd D. George U.S. Courthouse and Federal Building in Las Vegas in 2010 spurred efforts to improve judicial security.[78] An FY2005 supplemental appropriations act[79] included a provision that provided intrusion detection systems for judges in their homes, and the Court Security Improvement Act of 2007[80] aimed to enhance security for judges and court personnel as well as courtroom safety for the public.

The judiciary has been working closely with the U.S. Marshals Service (USMS) to ensure that adequate protective policies, procedures, and practices are in place. The FY2014 budget request would continue a pilot program for the USMS to assume responsibility for perimeter security at selected courthouses that were previously the responsibility of the Federal Protective Service (FPS). This pilot was first authorized in FY2009 as a result of the judiciary's stated concerns that FPS was not providing adequate perimeter security. After the initial planning phase, USMS implemented the pilot program on January 5, 2009, and assumed primary responsibility for security functions at seven courthouses located in Chicago, Detroit, Phoenix, New York, Tucson, and Baton Rouge (location of two of the seven courthouses). The judiciary and USMS have been evaluating the program and identifying areas for improvement. The judiciary reimburses USMS for the protective services.

---

[74] The Judicial Conference of the United States is the principal policymaking body for the federal courts system. The Chief Justice is the presiding officer of the conference, which comprises the chief judges of the 13 courts of appeals, a district judge from each of the 12 geographic circuits, and the chief judge of the Court of International Trade.

[75] Testimony of Honorable Julia S. Gibbons, Chair, Committee on the Budget of the Judicial Conference of the United States, in U.S. Congress, House Committee on Appropriations, Subcommittee on Financial Services and General Government, *Oversight Hearing - The Judiciary*, 113th Cong., 1st sess., March 20, 2013.

[76] Ibid., p. 3.

[77] For an analysis of court security and federal building security in general, see CRS Report R41138, *Federal Building, Courthouse, and Facility Security*, by Lorraine H. Tong and Shawn Reese.

[78] Steve Friess, "Two Killed in Las Vegas Courthouse," *The New York Times*, January 4, 2010, available at http://www.nytimes.com/2010/01/05/us/05vegas.html.

[79] P.L. 109-13.

[80] P.L. 110-177.

Supreme Court

The total FY2014 request for the Supreme Court, $86.5 million, was contained in two accounts: (1) Salaries and Expenses of $74.8 million and (2) Care of the Building and Grounds of $11.6 million.

The House-reported level of $74.2 million for the Salaries and Expenses account and $11.6 million for the Care of Building and Grounds account total $85.8 million. The House report indicated that the Care of Building and Grounds funding above the FY2013 level was for façade restoration. The Senate-reported level of $74.8 million for the Salaries and Expenses account and $11.2 million for the Care of Building and Grounds account total $86.0 million. The Senate report requires quarterly reports on the Supreme Court modernization project.

U.S. Court of Appeals for the Federal Circuit

This court, consisting of 12 judges, has jurisdiction and reviews, among other things, certain lower court rulings on patents and trademarks, international trade, and federal claims cases. The FY2014 budget request was $33.4 million. The House-reported bill would provide $30.9 million. The Senate-reported bill would provide $33.3 million.

U.S. Court of International Trade

This court has exclusive jurisdiction nationwide over the civil actions against the United States, its agencies and officers, and certain civil actions brought by the United States arising out of import transactions and the administration as well as enforcement of federal customs and international trade laws.

The FY2014 request was $22.0 million, while the House-reported level was $20.4 million, and the Senate-reported level was $21.4 million.

Courts of Appeals, District Courts, and Other Judicial Services

The FY2013 funding request of $6,822.9 million covers 12 of the 13 courts of appeals and 94 district judicial courts located in the 50 states, District of Columbia, Commonwealth of Puerto Rico, Commonwealth of the Northern Mariana Islands, and the territories of Guam and the U.S. Virgin Islands. The House-reported level was $6,643.8 million, while the Senate-reported level was $6,768.1 million. The account is divided among salaries and expenses, the Vaccine Injury Compensation Trust Fund, court security, defender services, and fees of jurors and commissioners.

Salaries and Expenses

The FY2014 request for this account is $5,170.2 million, while the House-reported level is $4,999.1 million and the Senate-reported level is $5,089.2 million.

Vaccine Injury Compensation Trust Fund

Established to address a perceived crisis in vaccine tort liability claims, the Vaccine Injury Compensation Program funds a federal no-fault program that protects the availability of vaccines in the nation by diverting a substantial number of claims from the tort arena. The FY2014 request was $5.3 million, while the House-reported level was $5.2 million, and the Senate-reported level was $5.4 million.

Court Security

This account provides for protective guard services, security systems, and equipment needs in courthouses and other federal facilities to ensure the safety of judicial officers, employees, and visitors. Under this account, the majority of funding for court security is transferred to the U.S. Marshals Service to pay for court security officers under the Judicial Facility Security Program. The FY2014 request was $524.3 million, while the House-reported bill would provide $520.0 million and the Senate-reported bill would provide $520.3 million.

Defender Services

This account funds the operations of the federal public defender and community defender organizations, and compensation, reimbursements, and expenses of private practice panel attorneys appointed by federal courts to serve as defense counsel to indigent individuals. The cost for this account is driven by the number and type of prosecutions brought by U.S. attorneys. The FY2014 request for these services was $1,068.6 million, while the House-reported bill would provide 1,065.0 million and the Senate-reported bill would provide $1,098.5 million. Both the House and Senate report stated that funding was not provided for an increase in the hourly panel attorney rate. The Senate report also contained language related to increased cost containment scrutiny for this account.

Fees of Jurors and Commissioners

This account funds the fees and allowances provided to grand and petit jurors, and compensation for jury and land commissioners. The FY2014 request was $54.4 million. The House-reported bill would provide funding at the requested level, while the Senate-reported bill would provide $54.9 million, which is $0.5 million greater than the budget request.

Administrative Office of the U.S. Courts

As the central support entity for the judiciary, the AOUSC provides a wide range of administrative, management, program, and information technology services to the U.S. courts. AOUSC also provides support to the Judicial Conference of the United States, and implements conference policies and applicable federal statutes and regulations. The FY2014 request for AOUSC was $85.4 million, the House-reported bill would provide $80.0 million, and the Senate-reported bill would provide $83.6 million.

Federal Judicial Center

As the judiciary's research and education entity, the Federal Judicial Center undertakes research and evaluation of judicial operations for the Judicial Conference committees and the courts. In addition, the center provides judges, court staff, and others with orientation and continuing education and training. The center's FY2014 request was $27.7 million, while the House-reported bill would provide $25.8 million and the Senate-reported bill would provide $26.4 million.

United States Sentencing Commission

The commission promulgates sentencing policies, practices, and guidelines for the federal criminal justice system. The FY2014 request was $17.0 million while the House-reported bill would provide $15.8 million and the Senate-reported bill would provide $16.6 million.

Judiciary Retirement Funds

This mandatory account provides for three trust funds that finance payments to retired bankruptcy and magistrate judges, retired Court of Federal Claims judges, and the spouses and dependent children of deceased judicial officers. The FY2014 request was for $126.9 million. Both the House and Senate would provide funding at the requested level. The House-reported bill provides for these funds in Title VI (General Provisions) of the FSGG bill, rather than in Title III (the Judiciary). The Senate-reported bill provides these funds in Title III of the bill.

Administrative Provisions

The House- and Senate-reported FSGG bills each contain new and continuing administrative provision language.

House Bill Language Continued from FY2013

- Section 301 would continue language to permit funds for salaries and expenses to be available for employment of experts and consultant services (as authorized by 5 U.S.C. §3109). (The judiciary also requested this section.)

- Section 302 would continue language to permit up to 5% of any appropriation made available for FY2013 to be transferred between judiciary appropriations accounts, provided that no appropriation would be decreased by more than 5% or increased by more than 10% by any such transfer, except in certain circumstances. In addition, the language would provide that any such transfer be treated as a reprogramming of funds under Sections 604 and 608 of the bill and would not be available for obligation or expenditure except in compliance with the procedures set forth in those sections. (The judiciary also requested this section.)

- Section 303 would continue language authorizing an amount not to exceed $11,000 to be used for official reception and representation expenses incurred by the Judicial Conference of the United States. (The judiciary also requested this section.)

- Section 304 would continue language to authorize a court security pilot program. (The judiciary also requested this section.)

House Proposed New Bill Language

- Section 305 would extend temporary judgeships.

- Section 306 would require a space management plan for reducing the number of square feet funded by the Court of Appeals, District Courts, and Other Judicial Services, Salaries and Expenses appropriation by FY2016.

Senate Bill Language Continued from FY2013

The Senate committee recommended the House bill language continued from FY2013 listed above, although Section 304 in the House bill is numbered Section 305 in the Senate bill.

Senate Proposed New Bill Language

- Senate Section 304 would grant the judicial branch the same tenant alteration authorities as the executive branch. The Senate included this language in FY2013.

- Senate Section 306 would provide certain contracting authorities to three judicial branch entities.

- Senate Section 307 would extend temporary judgeships.

- Senate Section 308 would authorize six additional district judgeships in response to increased caseloads and would convert two temporary judgeships, in California and Arizona, to permanent status.

District of Columbia[81]

The authority for congressional review and approval of the District of Columbia's budget is derived from the Constitution and the District of Columbia Self-Government and Government Reorganization Act of 1973 (the Home Rule Act).[82] The Constitution gave Congress the power to "exercise exclusive Legislation in all Cases whatsoever" pertaining to the District of Columbia. In 1973, Congress granted the city limited home rule authority and empowered citizens of the District to elect a mayor and city council. However, Congress retained the authority to review and approve all District laws, including the District's annual budget. As required by the Home Rule Act, the city council must approve a budget within 56 days after receiving a budget proposal from the mayor.[83] The approved budget must then be transmitted to the President, who forwards it to Congress for its review, possible modification, and approval.[84]

---

[81] This section authored by Eugene Boyd (x7-8689). For a more complete examination of appropriations for the District of Columbia, see CRS Report R43253, *FY2014 Appropriations: District of Columbia*, by Eugene Boyd.

[82] See Article I, Section 8, clause 17 of the U.S. Constitution; Section 446 of P.L. 93-198; 87 Stat. 801.

[83] 120 Stat. 2028.

[84] 87 Stat. 801.

District of Columbia appropriations acts typically include the following three components:

1. *Special federal payments* appropriated by Congress to be used to fund particular initiatives or activities of interest to Congress or the Administration.

2. The *District's operating budget*, including funds to cover the day-to-day functions, activities, and responsibilities of the District government; enterprise funds that provide for the operation and maintenance of District government facilities or services that are entirely or primarily supported by user-based fees; and long-term capital outlays such as road improvements. District operating budget expenditures are paid for by revenues generated through local taxes (sales and income), federal funds for which the District qualifies, and fees and other sources of funds.

3. *General provisions* are typically the third component of the District's budget reviewed and approved by Congress. These provisions can be grouped into several distinct but overlapping categories, with the most predominant being provisions relating to fiscal and budgetary directives and controls. Other provisions include administrative directives and controls, limitations on lobbying for statehood or congressional voting representation, congressional oversight, and congressionally imposed restrictions and prohibitions related to social policy.[85]

Both the President and Congress may propose financial assistance to the District in the form of "special federal payments" in support of specific activities or priorities. **Table 6** lists the pre-sequester amounts for FY2013, the President's FY2014 request, the District of Columbia's FY2014 request, and the amounts recommended by the House and Senate Appropriations Committees for FY2014.

Table 6. District of Columbia Special Federal Payments Appropriations, FY2013-FY2014

(in millions of dollars)

	FY2013 Pre-sequester	FY2014 Request	FY2014 District Request	FY2014 House Committee	FY2014 Senate Committee	FY2014 Enacted
Resident Tuition Support	$30	$35	$35	$15	$35	
Emergency Planning and Security	25	15	15	15	15	
District of Columbia Courts	232	223	223	233	232	
Defender Services	55	50	50	50	50	
Court Services and Offender	213	228	228	225	228	

[85] Congress has, from time to time, included language authorizing new programmatic initiatives or amendments to the District of Columbia home rule charter in the District's Appropriations bill. For example, in 1995, Congress included language authorizing the creation of public charter schools in the District of Columbia as part of P.L. 104-134, a consolidated appropriation measure. In 2004, Congress included statutory provisions creating a school voucher program as part of the District of Columbia Appropriations, which was a component of a consolidated appropriations act, P.L. 108-199.

	FY2013 Pre-sequester	FY2014 Request	FY2014 District Request	FY2014 House Committee	FY2014 Senate Committee	FY2014 Enacted
Supervision Agency						
Public Defender Service	37	41	41	39	41	
Criminal Justice Coordinating Council	2	2	2	2	2	
Judicial Commissions	0.5	0.5	0.5	0.5	0.5	
Water and Sewer Authority	15	15	15	—	15	
School Improvement	60	52	52	54	42	
Public Schools	*20*	*30*	*30*	*18*	*20*	
Public Charter Schools	*20*	*20*	*20*	*18*	*20*	
Education Vouchers-linked activities	*20*	*2*	*2*	*18*	*2*	
D.C. National Guard	0.4	0.5	0.5	0.4	0.5	
D.C. Comm. on Arts and Hum.	—	1	1	—		
St. Elizabeth Hospital Campus Redevelopment	—	10	10	—	10	
HIV/AIDS Prevention	5	5	5	3	5	
Special Federal Payments (total)	**$675**	**$676**	**$676**	**$637**	**$675**	

Sources: District of Columbia Fiscal Year 2014 Budget Request Act of 2013, A-20-0127; H.Rept. 113-172; and S.Rept. 113-80.

Note: Figures are rounded and columns may not sum due to rounding. "Pre-sequester FY2013" figures are from S.Rept. 113-80 and include across-the-board cuts under the Consolidated and Further Continuing Appropriations Act, 2013 (P.L. 113-6).

The President's Budget Request

On April 10, 2013, the Obama Administration released its detailed budget request for FY2014. The Administration's proposed budget included $676.3 million in special federal payments to the District of Columbia. Approximately 80% ($543.4 million) of the President's proposed budget request for the District would be targeted to the courts and criminal justice system. This included

- $222.7 million in support of court operations;

- $49.9 million for Defender Services;[86]

- $227.9 million for the Court Services and Offender Supervision Agency for the District of Columbia, an independent federal agency responsible for the District's pretrial services, adult probation, and parole supervision functions;

- $1.8 million for the Criminal Justice Coordinating Council;

- $40.6 million for the public defender's office;[87] and

- $500,000 to cover costs associated with investigating judicial misconduct complaints and recommending candidates to the President for vacancies to the District of Columbia Court of Appeals and the District of Columbia Superior Court.[88]

The President's budget request also included $87.2 million in support of education initiatives, with $52.2 million to support elementary and secondary education, $500,000 to support the D.C. National Guard college access program, and $35 million for college tuition assistance. These amounts represented 12.9% of the Administration's federal payment budget request for the District of Columbia.

The District's FY2014 Budget

On March 28, 2013, the mayor of the District of Columbia submitted a proposed budget to the District of Columbia Council, the "Fiscal Year 2014 Budget Request Act of 2013." On May 22, 2013, the council approved a FY2014 budget that included $12.2 billion in proposed operating funds, $2.2 billion in proposed capital outlays, and $676 million in proposed special federal payments. The mayor signed the measure (A20-0127) on July 24, 2013. Included in the act were provisions to grant the District greater self-governance, providing some level of budget autonomy in the expenditure of local funds and legislative autonomy. Specifically, the act would, by reference, enact the "Local Budget Autonomy Act of 2012."[89] The budget act, if approved by Congress, would thus amend the District's home rule charter by removing language that currently subjects the District's general fund budget to the congressional appropriations process. Specifically, under the Local Budget Autonomy Act, the District's local budget would become effective if Congress failed to enact a joint resolution of disapproval within a 30-day

---

[86] Funds are administered by the Joint Committee on Judicial Administration in the District of Columbia and may be used to provide court appointed attorneys and other services for (1) indigent persons charged with a criminal offense; (2) family proceedings in which child neglect is alleged, or where the termination of the parent-child relationship is under consideration; and (3) the representation and protection of mentally incapacitated individuals and minors whose parents are deceased. Funds may also be used to provide guardian training and payments for counsel appointed in adoption proceedings, and for services such as transcripts of court proceedings, expert witness testimony, foreign and sign language interpretation, investigations, and genetic testing.

[87] The Public Defender Service for the District of Columbia is a federally funded, independent organization governed by an eleven-member Board of Trustees. Created by federal statute (P.L. 91-358; D.C. Code Section 2-1601), the Public Defender Service implements the constitutional mandate to provide criminal defense counsel for indigent individuals. The organization also provides legal representation for individuals facing involuntary civil commitment in the District's mental health system or parole revocation for D.C. Code offenses.

[88] This includes $295,000 to the Commission on Judicial Disabilities and Tenure and $205,000 to the Judicial Nomination Commission.

[89] D.C. Act 19-632, which would have amended the District's Home Rule Act, subject to approval by voter referendum.

---

congressional review period. Thus, the District's local budget would no longer require active approval by Congress.[90]

In addition to budget autonomy, the District's Fiscal Year 2014 Budget Request Act of 2013 included several provisions intended to advance legislative autonomy. The act would:

- eliminate the requirement that proposed amendments to the District's home rule charter be transmitted to Congress;

- no longer subject proposed charter amendments to the 35-day congressional review period;

- no longer subject the District's borrowing authority to the congressional appropriations process; and

- shorten the congressional review period (which currently allows Congress 30 legislative days to review non-criminal-code legislation passed by the District of Columbia Council and 60 days for legislation related to criminal offenses, procedures, and prisoners) by eliminating language that excludes Saturdays, Sundays, holidays, and any day on which neither chamber is in session because of an adjournment sine die, a recess of more than 3 days, or an adjournment of more than 3 days beginning on the day the legislation is transmitted to the House or Senate.

House Measure (H.R. 2786)

H.R. 2786 as reported by the House Committee on Appropriations includes $637 million in special federal payments to the District. This is $395 million less than requested by the Obama Administration and $38 million less than recommended by the Senate bill. The House bill would not include funding for the District's Water and Sewer Authority and includes a substantial decrease ($20 million) in the amount to be appropriated for the Resident Tuition Support (college access) program. The bill also would direct $54 million in funding to support the District of Columbia Public Schools ($18 million), public charter schools ($18 million), and private school vouchers ($18 million).

General Provisions

The House bill included several general provisions governing budgetary and fiscal operations and controls including prohibiting deficit spending within budget accounts, establishing restrictions on the reprogramming of funds, and allowing the transfer of local funds to capital and enterprise

---

[90] This is an alternative to a provision that was included in the District's FY2013 budget request. That proposal would have granted the District some level of budget autonomy in the expenditure of local funds if Congress failed to pass, and the President failed sign, a District of Columbia appropriations act before the beginning of FY2013. The provision would have allowed the District to obligate and expend local funds at the rate set forth in the act during the period in which there is an absence of a federal appropriations act authorizing the expenditure of local funds. Similar language was included in a Senate bill (S. 3301,112[th] Congress) recommending appropriations for FY2013 as reported by the Senate Appropriations Committee. (See S. 3301, Title VIII, §815.) The provision was also supported by the Administration. (See Executive Office of the President, U.S. President (Obama), "Statement of Administration Policy: H.R. 6020 – Financial Services and General Government Appropriations Act, 2013", June 28, 2012), p. 4, at http://www.whitehouse.gov/sites/default/files/omb/legislative/sap/112/saphr6020r_20120628.pdf.)

fund accounts. In addition, the bill would require the city's Chief Financial Officer to submit a revised operating budget for all District government agencies and the District public schools within 30 days after the passage of the bill.

The House bill also includes several general provisions relating to statehood or congressional representation for the District, including provisions that would continue prohibiting the use of *federal funds* to

- support or defeat any legislation being considered by Congress or a state legislature;

- cover salaries, expenses, and other costs associated with the office of Statehood Representative and Statehood Senator for the District of Columbia; and

- support efforts by the District of Columbia Attorney General or any other officer of the District government to provide assistance for any petition drive or civil action seeking voting representation in Congress for citizens of the District.

H.R. 2786 would prohibit the use of both District and federal funds for abortion services. In addition, the bill would continue to prohibit the use of federal funds to administer needle exchange or to decriminalize or regulate the medical use of marijuana. Despite the federal prohibition, on June 12, 2012, the city announced the certification of four privately operated medical marijuana dispensaries.[91] The first dispensary opened on July 29, 2013.[92]

Senate Measure (S. 1371)

S. 1371 as reported by the Senate Committee on Appropriations would provide for $675 million in special federal payments to the District. This is approximately $1 million less than requested by the Administration. The bill included $9.4 million more in funding for court operations than requested by the Administration. It would appropriate $10 million less than the President's FY2014 request for elementary and secondary education initiatives. These funds would be allocated among three specific initiatives: public school improvements ($20 million), support for public charter schools ($20 million), and funding a private school voucher program ($2.2 million for evaluation and administration activities). The Senate report accompanying the bill noted that there are sufficient unexpended funds available from pervious appropriations to meet the needs of the school voucher program.

General Provisions

The Senate bill's general provisions mirror some of the language included in the House bill. Like the House bill, S. 1371 included provisions governing budgetary and fiscal operations and

---

[91] District of Columbia Department of Health, "DC Department of Health Notifies Applicants Eligible to Register for Medical Marijuana Dispensaries," press release, June 12, 2012, at http://newsroom.dc.gov/show.aspx/agency/doh/section/2/release/23453/year/2012.

[92] Ryan J. Reilly and Nick Wing, "Washington, D.C.'s First Medical Marijuana Dispensary Opens Blocks From Capitol," *Huffington Post*, July 30, 2013, at http://www.huffingtonpost.com/2013/07/30/washington-dc-medical-marijuana-dispensary_n_3676943.html.

controls. It also included provisions restricting or prohibiting the use of federal funds to support District statehood or congressional voting representation and included provisions that would continue prohibiting the use of *federal funds* to

- support or defeat any legislation being considered by Congress or a state legislature;

- cover salaries, expenses and other costs associated with the office of Statehood Representative and Statehood Senator for the District of Columbia; and

- support efforts by the District of Columbia Attorney General or any other officer of the District government to provide assistance for any petition drive or civil action seeking voting representation in Congress for citizens of the District.

The bill also included changes in three provisions that city officials have sought to eliminate or modify. The bill would

- continue the prohibition against the use of federal funds to provide abortion services;

- prohibit the use of federal funds to regulate and decriminalize the medical use of marijuana; and

- maintain the current prohibition on the use of federal funds to support a needle exchange program.

The Senate bill included provisions not included in previous District of Columbia appropriations acts passed by Congress that would amend the District's home rule charter. The Senate measure would grant the city fiscal year and budget autonomy over the expenditure of locally raised funds, an action long sought by District officials. Specifically, the Senate measure would decouple the District's fiscal year from the federal fiscal year and would grant the District the authority to spend local funds if Congress has not enacted a federal appropriation authorizing the expenditure of local funds before the start of the District's fiscal year.

Funding Lapse

To mitigate the impact of congressional delays in the approval of the District's appropriation before the beginning of a fiscal year, Congress has routinely included language in continuing budget resolutions allowing the District to expend local funds on programs and activities included in its General Fund budget. Before the beginning of FY2014, Congress did not approve the District of Columbia Appropriation for FY2014 or a continuing resolution. In response to the funding lapse, the District used a $144 million contingency fund to keep the city operating. On October 2, 2013, the House considered and passed H.J.Res. 71, the District of Columbia Continuing Appropriations Resolution, 2014, which would have allowed the District to use locally raised revenues to fund District operations through December 15, 2013, though the Senate did not act on this measure. Ultimately the District was provided funding until January 15, 2014 under the Continuing Appropriations Act, 2014 (H.R. 2775, P.L. 113-46).

ᵻnᵡeᵡenᵡent ᵡᵡenᵡes

The FSGG appropriations bill provides funding for more than two dozen independent agencies performing a wide range of functions. These functions include the management of federal real property (GSA), the regulation of financial institutions and markets (SEC and CFTC), and mail delivery (USPS). **Table 7** lists the pre-sequester amounts for FY2013, the President's FY2014 request, and the amounts recommended by the House and Senate appropriations committees for FY2014.

Table 7. Independent Agencies Appropriations, FY2013-FY2014

(in millions of dollars)

Agency	FY2013 Pre-sequester	FY2014 Request	FY2014 House Committee	FY2014 Senate Committee	FY2014 Enacted
Administrative Conference of the United States	$3	$3	—	$3	
Christopher Columbus Fellowship Foundation	0.5	—	—	0.2	
Civilian Property Realignment Board	—	17	—	—	
Commodity Futures Trading Commission[a]	205	315	195	315	
Consumer Product Safety Commission	114	117	114	117	
Election Assistance Commission	12	11	—	11	
Federal Communications Commission[b]	(340)	(360)	(320)	360	
Federal Deposit Insurance Corporation: Office of Inspector General (by transfer)[c]	(35)	(35)	(35)	(35)	
Federal Election Commission	66	66	66	66	
Federal Labor Relations Authority	25	25	24	25	
Federal Trade Commission	181	183	176	89	
General Services Administration[d]	-1,433	248	-2,185	248	
Harry S Truman Scholarship Foundation	1	—	—	1	
Merit Systems Protection Board	43	42	42	45	
Morris K. Udall Foundation	6	6	—	6	
National Archives and Records Administration	374	368[e]	366	370	
National Credit Union Administration	1	1	1	1	
Office of Government Ethics	19	15	15	15	
Office of Personnel Management (total)	20,883	20,875	20,871	20,875	
Office of Special Counsel	19	21	21	21	
Postal Regulatory Comm.	14	14	14	14	

Agency	FY2013 Pre-sequester	FY2014 Request	FY2014 House Committee	FY2014 Senate Committee	FY2014 Enacted
Privacy and Civil Liberties Oversight Board[f]	1	3	3	4	
Recovery and Accountability Transparency Board	28	13	20	20	
Securities and Exchange Commission[b]	(1,321)	(1,674)	(1,371)	(1,674)	
Selective Service System	24	24	24	23	
Small Business Administration	1,847	969	897	949	
SBA Disaster Relief Appropriations	804	—	—	—	
United States Postal Service	310	312	311	312	
United States Tax Court	51	53	51	53	
Total: Independent Agencies	**$22,809**	**$23,685**	**$20,944**	**$23,585**	

Sources: H.Rept. 113-172; S.Rept. 113-80; and H.Rept. 113-116.

Notes: All figures are rounded, and columns also may not equal the total due to rounding. "Pre-sequester FY2013" figures are from S.Rept. 113-80 and include across-the-board cuts under the Consolidated and Further Continuing Appropriations Act, 2013 (P.L. 113-6).

a. The CFTC is funded in the House through the Agriculture appropriations bill and in the Senate through the Financial Services and General Government bill.

b. The FCC and the SEC received all of their FY2012 funding through the collection of regulatory fees, resulting in no direct appropriation. Therefore, the amounts shown for the FCC and SEC represent budgetary resources made available by Congress, but those amounts are not included in the table totals.

c. Budget authority transferred to FDIC is not included in total FSGG appropriations; it is counted as part of the budget authority in the appropriation account from which it came.

d. GSA's real property activities are funded through the Federal Buildings Fund (FBF), a multi-billion dollar revolving fund into which rental payments from federal agencies that lease GSA space are deposited. Revenue in the FBF is then made available by Congress each year to pay for GSA's real property activities. A negative total for the FBF occurs when the amount of funds made available for expenditure in a fiscal year is less than the amount of new revenue expected to be deposited.

e. Amount as shown in S.Rept. 113-80; it does not include appropriations for repayments of principal on the construction of the Archives II facility. The amount reported in the President's budget request, $385.8 million, includes this principal repayment.

f. The House recommended no funding for FY2013 and a $1 million rescission of prior year unobligated balances.

*ureau *****nsu* er *han**a***te*t*n[93]

The Dodd-Frank Act created a Bureau of Consumer Financial Protection (popularly known as the Consumer Financial Protection Bureau or CFPB) as an independent agency with funding from the Federal Reserve that is, by statute, not subject to review by the House and Senate Appropriations Committees. Neither the President's budget request nor S. 1371 as reported contain changes to the underlying CFPB law and neither would appropriate funds for the bureau. In contrast, H.R. 2786

---

[93] For more information on the CFPB, see CRS Report R42572, *The Consumer Financial Protection Bureau (CFPB): A Legal Analysis*, by David H. Carpenter.

as reported includes legislative language that would prohibit any transfer of funds from the Federal Reserve to the CFPB as of October 1, 2014, instead authorizing regular appropriations for the CFBP. The bill would also require regular notification and reports by the CFPB to the House and Senate Committees on Appropriations as well as the relevant authorizing committees through FY2014.

Civilian Property Realignment Board[94]

The President requested $17.0 million for a new Civilian Property Realignment Board (CPRB), which would develop recommendations as to which civilian federal properties should be consolidated, reconfigured, redeveloped, leased, sold, or conveyed. No funding was provided in FY2012 or FY2013, and neither the House nor the Senate Appropriations Committees recommended funding for FY2014.[95]

Commodity Futures Trading Commission[96]

The Commodity Futures Trading Commission (CFTC) is the independent regulatory agency charged with oversight of derivatives markets. The CFTC's functions include oversight of trading on the futures exchanges, registration and supervision of futures industry personnel, prevention of fraud and price manipulation, and investor protection. Although most futures trading is now related to financial variables (interest rates, currency prices, and stock indexes), congressional authorization jurisdiction remains vested in the House and Senate Agriculture Committees because of the market's historical origins as an adjunct to agricultural markets. Appropriations for the CFTC are under the jurisdiction of the Agriculture Appropriations Subcommittee in the House, and the Financial Services and General Government Appropriations Subcommittee in the Senate. The President requested, and the Senate Appropriations Committee recommended, $315.0 million for FY2014, while the House Appropriations Committee recommended $194.6 million.

Consumer Product Safety Commission[97]

The Consumer Product Safety Commission (CPSC) is an independent federal regulatory agency whose mission is to reduce the risk of harm in the use of consumer products. In carrying out its statutory responsibilities, the commission creates mandatory safety standards for products to lower the risk of injury to consumers; works with industries to develop voluntary safety standards; bans products it deems unsafe when voluntary safety standards are not feasible; monitors recalls of defective products; informs and educates consumers about product hazards; conducts research on and develops testing methods for product safety; collects and publishes data

---

[94] This section authored by Garrett Hatch (x7-7822). For more information on federal real property reform legislation, see CRS Report R43247, *Disposal of Unneeded Federal Buildings: Legislative Proposals in the 113th Congress*, by Garrett Hatch.

[95] One bill, the Civilian Property Realignment Act of 2013 (H.R. 695), has been introduced in the 113th Congress to establish such a board and provide it with funding. H.R. 695 would authorize $82 million in funding for the CPRB.

[96] For more information on the CFTC, see CRS Report R43117, *The Commodity Futures Trading Commission: Background and Current Issues*, by Rena S. Miller.

[97] This section authored by Gary Guenther (x7-7742).

on injuries and product hazards; and promotes uniform product regulations among state and local governments.

In FY2013, prior to the sequester, the CPSC was to receive $114.3 million in appropriated funds, nearly the same as the amount enacted for FY2012. CPSC's funding has increased significantly since FY2007, when it totaled about $62.0 million. From FY2008 through FY2010, Congress approved significant increases in funding for the agency, largely to support major reforms initiated by the Consumer Product Safety Improvement Act of 2008(CPSIA). [98] The 110th Congress passed this act partly in response to a series of highly publicized recalls of imported products, particularly unsafe toys and other items manufactured for children. Among other things, the act enhanced the commission's recall authority, simplified the rulemaking process, established a new searchable database for consumer product complaints, and mandated product certification.

The President's Budget Request

For FY2014, the CPSC requested $117.0 million in appropriations. Of this amount, $75.4 million would go to employee compensation (including benefits). Viewed from the perspective of CPSC's strategic goals and programs, the budget request allocated $30.4 million to hazard identification and reduction; $24.1 million to compliance and field operations; $4.6 million to import surveillance; $2.2 million to education, global outreach, and small business; $18.4 million to information technology; and $21.3 million to agency management, rent, and security.

The budget request also encompassed several proposed investments. [99] Specifically, the CPSC proposed spending $2.0 million to continue its participation in an interagency effort known as the National Nanotechnology Initiative; $1.1 million to operate the National Product Testing and Evaluation Center, which opened in 2011; $2.1 million to operate a database on injuries caused by products and treated in hospital emergency rooms known as the National Emergency Injury Surveillance System; $2.7 million on the operation and maintenance of the Consumer Product Safety Risk Management System; $0.9 million on its consumer hotline; $1.9 million on a pilot program to determine the effectiveness of a method for identifying imports of consumer products that may violate U.S. safety laws and regulations; $16.2 million for field investigators; and $1.0 million for a pool safety and education program authorized by the Virginia Graeme Baker Pool and Spa Safety Act. [100]

House Measure (H.R. 2786)

H.R. 2786 as reported by the House Committee on Appropriations would provide for an appropriation of $114.0 million for the CPSC in FY2014, 2.6% less than the budget request. Of that amount, $500,000 was designated for the grant program established by the Virginia Graeme Baker Pool and Spa Safety Act; the funds would be available until they are spent or obligated.

In its report on H.R. 2786, the committee pointed out the advantages of the CPSC establishing cooperative relationships with the private sector in seeking the voluntary recall of products the commission deems hazardous. It also expressed support for the agency's Import Safety Initiative,

---

[98] P.L. 110-314.

[99] For more details on the request, see http://www.cpsc.gov/cpscpub/pubs/reports/2013plan.pdf.

[100] P.L. 110-140.

which enables the CPSC to station investigators at key ports to prevent hazardous products from entering the United States.

Section 628 of the bill would require the GAO to undertake a cost-benefit analysis of the changes the CPSIA made in the CPSC's mission and operations. Although a CPSIA reform bill[101] enacted in August 2011 addressed some of the committee's concerns about lead limits in certain consumer products and third-party testing requirements, the committee indicated that the reforms did not go far enough and believed a study of the impact of the CPSIA is warranted.

The committee also encouraged the CPSC to continue its partnership with manufacturers of window covers to educate consumers about the potential hazards of window cover cords.

Senate Measure (S. 1371)

S. 1371 as reported by the Senate Committee on Appropriations would provide that the CPSC receive $117.0 million in appropriations in FY2014.

In its report on S. 1371, the committee expressed its support for the commission's efforts under the CPSIA to ensure that current safety standards for durable infant and toddler products and chemicals are appropriately stringent. It also opposed any move in Congress to "impose additional statutory constraints" on those efforts.

The committee urged the CPSC to take action to reduce the use of flame-retardant chemicals, particularly in furniture, and to continue working on a standard for furniture flammability that takes into consideration the risk of "smoldering ignition" and does not interfere with the eventual adoption by California of a proposed new standard.

Section 502 of the bill would require the GAO to conduct a study of the commission's ability to respond quickly to emerging product hazards.

Election Assistance Commission[102]

The Election Assistance Commission (EAC) was established under the Help America Vote Act of 2002(HAVA).[103] The commission provides grant funding to the states to meet the HAVA requirements and for election reform programs; provides for testing and certification of voting machines; issues studies of election issues; and promulgates voluntary guidelines for voting systems standards and issues voluntary guidance with respect to the act's requirements. Although the commission was not given new rulemaking authority under HAVA, the law transferred responsibilities for the National Voter Registration Act (NVRA),[104] including NVRA rule-making authority, from the Federal Election Commission to the EAC. The Department of Justice is charged with enforcement responsibility under HAVA.

---

[101] P.L. 112-28.

[102] This section authored by Kevin Coleman (x7-7878).

[103] P.L. 107-252; 116 Stat. 1666.

[104] P.L. 103-31.

The President's budget request for FY2014 included $11.0 million for the EAC, of which $2.75 million is to be transferred to the National Institute of Standards and Technology (NIST) to support work on testing guidelines for voting system hardware and software.

The House Committee on Appropriations recommended eliminating the EAC and transferring its functions to the Federal Election Commission; therefore, the committee provides no funding for the agency for FY2014. The House committee report noted that all statutorily mandated agency positions are vacant, all appropriated funds have been distributed, and the Administration has not requested additional funds in three years. In addition, the President appointed an ad hoc commission to review the 2012 election and make recommendations, rather than directing the EAC to do so.[105]

The Senate Committee on Appropriations recommended providing $11.0 million for EAC operations, of which $2.75 million is to be transferred to NIST. The committee report directed the Director of NIST to provide an expenditure plan to the EAC and the committee within 30 days of the transfer and directed the EAC and NIST to set priorities to meet timelines for the related work.

Federal Communications Commission[106]

The Federal Communications Commission (FCC) is an independent federal agency with its five members appointed by the President, subject to confirmation by the Senate. It was established by the Communications Act of 1934[107] (1934 Act or "Communications Act") and is charged with regulating interstate and international communications by radio, television, wire, satellite, and cable. The statutory purpose of the FCC is to ensure that the American people have available, "without discrimination on the basis of race, color, religion, national origin, or sex, a rapid, efficient, Nation-wide, and world-wide wire and radio communication service with adequate facilities at reasonable charges."

Most or all of the FCC's budget is derived from regulatory fees collected by the agency rather than through a direct appropriation. The fees, often referred to as "Section (9) fees," are collected from license holders and certain other entities (e.g., cable television systems) and deposited into an FCC account. The law gives the FCC authority to review the regulatory fees and to adjust the fees to reflect changes in its appropriation from year to year. Most years, appropriations language prohibits the use by the commission of any excess collections received in the current fiscal year or any prior years. These funds remain in the FCC account and are not made available to other agencies or agency programs or redirected into the Treasury's general fund.

---

[105] The House committee noted its support for legislation in the 113th Congress to eliminate the EAC (H.R. 1994) and for similar legislation passed by the House in the previous Congress.

[106] This section authored by Patricia Moloney Figliola, Specialist in Internet and Telecommunications Policy, Resources, Science, and Industry Division.

[107] 47 U.S.C. §151 *et seq.*

✶✶e ✶✶✶✶ ✶u✶✶et ✶e✶uest

For FY2014, the FCC requested a budget of $359.3 million, with no direct appropriation (i.e., the entire budget will be funded through auction proceeds).[108] It included requests for funding to

- support commission-wide information technology needs through extending the enterprise storage;

- support for reform of the Universal Service Fund Support Program;

- space consolidation and facilities improvement that will reduce lease arrangements that are not cost effective and improve efficiencies;

- create a Do-Not-Call registry for telephone numbers used by Public Safety Answering Points;

- provide resources for mission-critical systems to ensure that they are operational during a Continuity of Operations event; and

- provide contract funding to support mandatory audits for the Office of the Inspector General. The budget submission also included a request to decrease the spending of Auctions funding from $98.7 million to $89.4 million to support the timely implementation of the Auctions Incentive program.

✶✶use Measure (✶.✶. ✶7✶✶)

H.R. 2786 as reported by the House Committee on Appropriations provided for an FCC appropriation of $320 million for FY 2014, all of which is to be derived from the collection of offsetting collections. This amount is $39.3 million less than the request.[109]

The House committee noted that it believes the current organizational and management structure of the commission does not reflect the technological development that has resulted in the convergence of today's telecommunications market. It stated that the increase in market-based competition should lead to a smaller commission, reorganized to address the current market. The committee directed the commission to submit within 180 days of enactment a review of its organizational structure as well as a proposal for improvement that reflects today's technology landscape and competitive marketplace.

The committee also directed the commission to submit within 30 days of enactment, and thereafter annually in its annual budget submission, a detailed justification to the Committees on Appropriations in the House and Senate as to how the commission intends to spend funds raised in the incentive auctions called for in Title VI of the Middle Class Tax Relief and Job Creation Act of 2012.[110]

---

[108] See http://www.fcc.gov/document/fcc-fy-2014-budget.

[109] The request also allows, among other items: (1) collection of $320,000,000 in section 9 fees; (2) a prohibition on amounts collected in excess of $320,000,000 from being available for obligation; (3) a prohibition on remaining prior year offsetting collections from being available for obligation; and (4) a cap of $89,400,000 for the administration and implementation of incentive auctions, as required by P.L. 112-96.

[110] P.L. 112-96.

Senate Measure (S. 1371)

S. 1371 as reported by the Senate Committee on Appropriations provides for a budget of $359.3 million for FY 2014, all of which would be derived from the collection of offsetting fees. This amount was equal to the budget request.

The bill includes language to extend the FCC's exemption from the Anti-deficiency Act until December 31, 2015 (Section 510), and prohibit the FCC from enacting certain recommendations regarding universal service that were made by the Joint Board of FCC members and state utility commissioners (Section 511).

The committee report directed the FCC to develop a plan to fully implement its Statement of Policy on Establishing a Government-to-Government Relationship with Indian tribes that it adopted in June 2000 and to report to the committee if it needs resources to do so.

The committee expressed concern regarding the persistence of calls failing to complete to rural areas because of the potential threat to public safety and local economies and directed the FCC to submit a report to the Committee within 60 days of enactment detailing (1) the process and extent to which it is tracking call completion rates, (2) how the FCC is reviewing anomalies in call completion rates, and (3) what steps the FCC plans to take to resolve call completion problems.

Federal Deposit Insurance Corporation Office of the Inspector General[111]

The FDIC's Office of the Inspector General is funded from deposit insurance funds; the OIG has no direct support from federal taxpayers. Before FY1998, the amount was approved by the FDIC Board of Directors; the amount is now directly appropriated (through a transfer) to ensure the independence of the OIG.

For FY2014, the President requested, and the House and Senate Appropriations Committees recommended, an appropriation of $34.6 million.

Federal Election Commission[112]

The FEC is an independent agency that administers, and enforces civil compliance with, the Federal Election Campaign Act[113] (FECA) and campaign finance regulations. The agency does so through educational outreach, rulemaking, and litigation, and by issuing advisory opinions. The FEC also administers the presidential public financing system.[114] In recent years, FEC

---

[111] This section authored by Darryl Getter (x7-2834). For more information on the FDIC, see CRS Report R41718, *Federal Deposit Insurance for Banks and Credit Unions*, by Darryl E. Getter.

[112] This section authored by R. Sam Garrett (x7-6443).

[113] 2 U.S.C. §431 *et seq.*

[114] The Treasury Department and IRS also have administrative responsibilities for presidential public financing. However, Congress does not appropriate funds for the program. For additional discussion, see CRS Report RL34534, *Public Financing of Presidential Campaigns: Overview and Analysis*, by R. Sam Garrett.

appropriations have generally been noncontroversial and subject to limited debate in committee or on the House and Senate floors.[115]

For FY2014, the President requested $65.8 million for the FEC. As in previous years, approximately 90% of the FEC budget is expected to be accounted for by three major expense areas: (1) salaries and benefits, (2) rent, and (3) information technology (IT).[116] Although personnel and rent expenditures are relatively fixed, IT expenditures can vary. They have been consistently prominent in recent years and are again expected to be a major part of the agency's budget in 2014. Among other points, this includes adapting the FEC's widely used filing software, FECFILE, to a web-based platform and other technology upgrades to maintain the agency's campaign finance disclosure responsibilities. These efforts, initiated in FY2012 and FY2013, remain ongoing priorities.[117] The agency also faces a backlog of enforcement cases requiring processing. Most of these cases originated during the 2012 election cycle.[118] The FEC also expects to focus on human resources issues during FY2014, including allocating staff to handle the increased enforcement caseload and implementation of a new performance appraisal system.[119]

The House Appropriations Committee recommended an FY2014 appropriation of $65.8 million, the same amount as requested. The House committee report and legislative language contained no additional instructions except a $5,000 limit on "reception and representation," a prohibition that has long been included in FEC appropriations provisions. Elsewhere, the committee report recommended transferring some Election Assistance Commission (EAC) duties to the FEC.[120]

The Senate Appropriations Committee recommended an FY2014 appropriation of $66.4 million, $600,000 more than the President's request. Accompanying report language noted that Section 621 of the Senate bill would require Senate political committees to file disclosure reports electronically—thus reporting under the same standard as all other federal political committees.[121] The Senate report did not otherwise include instructions for the agency.

Other sections of the FSGG bills may also be relevant for campaign finance matters. In particular, Section 735 of the House measure contains a prohibition on requiring government contractors to provide information about their or their employees' federal campaign contributions, electioneering communications, or independent expenditures as a condition of receiving the contract. Title V of the bill ("government-wide policy") would similarly prohibit spending certain federal funds on information technology used to track corporate independent expenditures, electioneering communications, or related activities. As CRS has noted elsewhere, the Obama Administration has reportedly considered issuing an executive order to require additional disclosure of government contractors' political expenditures. No such order has been issued, but

---

[115] For additional discussion of current campaign finance issues, see CRS Report R41542, *The State of Campaign Finance Policy: Recent Developments and Issues for Congress*, by R. Sam Garrett.

[116] Federal Election Commission, *FY2014 Congressional Budget Justification* (Washington: April 2013), p. 6, available at http://www.fec.gov/pages/budget/fy2014/fy_2014_cbj_%204-10-13_final.pdf.

[117] Federal Election Commission, *FY2014 Congressional Budget Justification*, pp. 1-2.

[118] Federal Election Commission, *FY2014 Congressional Budget Justification*, pp. 2-3.

[119] Federal Election Commission, *FY2014 Congressional Budget Justification*, pp. 8-9.

[120] H.Rept. 113-172, pp. 46-47.

[121] S.Rept. 113-80, p. 82. For additional discussion, see CRS Report R41542, *The State of Campaign Finance Policy: Recent Developments and Issues for Congress*, by R. Sam Garrett.

several measures have proposed barring the disclosure reportedly under consideration.[122] Finally, although other sections of the bill contain provisions related to campaign finance matters, such as restrictions on Securities and Exchange Commission reporting of political expenditures, or Internal Revenue Service restrictions, these provisions are not directly relevant for the FEC and are not addressed in this section.

Federal Trade Commission[123]

The Federal Trade Commission (FTC) is an independent agency whose mission is to protect consumers and maintain or enhance competition in a broad range of industries. It does so mainly by enforcing laws that bar anticompetitive, deceptive, or unfair business practices, and by educating consumers and business owners to foster informed consumer choices, compliance with the law, and a better understanding of the competitive process.

Operating funds for the agency come from three sources, listed here in descending order of importance: (1) direct appropriations, (2) pre-merger filing fees under the Hart-Scott-Rodino Antitrust Improvements Act of 1976,[124] and (3) Do-Not-Call Registry fees.

The President's Budget Request

For FY2014, the President requested $182.7 million in direct appropriations for the FTC. Hart-Scott-Rodino pre-merger filing fees are expected to yield $103.0 million, and Do-Not-Call fees may add $15 million, giving the FTC a total appropriation of $301.0 million in FY2014 under the request.

In keeping with the FTC's mission, its budget is divided between resources for protecting consumers and resources for maintaining competition. Under the FY2014 budget request, 56.5% of available resources would go to the former purpose, while 43.5% would support the latter purpose. Within these broad functional categories, the budget request is intended to enable the agency to undertake a variety of planned activities in FY2014 and beyond, including

- protecting consumers from fraudulent practices in the financial services market;
- protecting consumer privacy in online transactions;
- combating identity theft;
- monitoring the advertising of health-care products for false or deceptive claims;
- protecting children from unfair and deceptive marketing;
- promoting competition in health care services and pharmaceuticals;
- challenging anti-competitive mergers;
- preventing anti-competitive practices in the energy industry;

---

[122] See CRS Report R41542, *The State of Campaign Finance Policy: Recent Developments and Issues for Congress*, by R. Sam Garrett.

[123] This section authored by Gary Guenther (x7-7742).

[124] P.L. 94-435.

- increasing its efforts to keep consumers and businesses informed about the benefits of competition; and

- enforcing FTC orders.

Included in the budget request are a decrease of $26.4 million related to efficiencies in the replacement of office space and increases of $5.5 million for mandatory expenses such as pay adjustments, $10.3 million for new IT investments, and $1.0 million for increased witness costs related to anti-competitive activities and rising consumer demand for the Sentinel Network Services.

✱✱use Measure (✱.✱. ✱7✱✱)

H.R. 2786 as reported by the House Committee on Appropriations provided for a direct appropriation of $176.7 million for the FTC in FY2014, 3.2% less than the budget request. This amount would be supplemented by an estimated $103.3 million in Hart-Scott-Rodino pre-merger filing fees and $15 million in Do-Not-Call fees for a total appropriation of $295.0 million in FY2014.

In its report on the bill, the committee noted that jurisdiction for some of the areas of consumer protection previously handled exclusively by the FTC was transferred to the Consumer Financial Protection Bureau by the Dodd-Frank Act. Under a Memorandum of Understanding signed by the two agencies, the FTC and the CFPB have agreed to consult on matters of common jurisdiction, such as debt collection. The committee expected the FTC to do its part to avoid duplicating any rulemaking by the CFPB.[125]

Senate Measure (S. 1371)

S. 1371 as reported by the Senate Committee on Appropriations would provide a direct appropriation of $89.0 for the FTC in FY2014, 51.4% below the budget request. This amount would be supplemented by an estimated $197 million in Hart-Scott-Rodino pre-merger filing fees and $15 million in Do-Not-Call fees, leaving a total appropriation of $301.0 million in FY2014.

Section 624 of the bill would adjust the pre-merger filing fees for inflation for the first time since 2001 and establish a new tier in the fee structure for merger transactions valued at more than $1 million. Under current law, there are three tiers of pre-merger filing fees, and they apply to transactions valued at $70.9 million and above. Adding the proposed new tier would subject transactions valued at more than $1 million to the fees, increasing the total amount of fees collected annually. This explains why the Senate committee's estimate of pre-merger filing fees for FY2014 was $94 million greater than the estimate used in both the budget request and the House Appropriations Committee's budget recommendation.

In its report on S. 1371, the committee commended the commission for its ongoing efforts to protect consumers from fraudulent practices related to identity theft, mortgage lending, data security, and health care. In addition, the committee expressed appreciation for the FTC's efforts to preserve competition in the marketplace through disseminating information on and enforcing federal anti-trust statutes. It directed the commission to "robustly" continue these activities.

---

[125] H.Rept. 113-172, p. 51.

The committee also expected the FTC to continue its efforts to enforce the Children's Online Privacy Protection Act of 1998[126] and to carefully monitor agreements between generic drug producers and brand-name drug producers to keep generic versions of branded drugs off the market or delay their entry for their potential impact on consumer welfare and competition in the market for those drugs.

General Services Administration[127]

The General Services Administration (GSA) administers federal civilian procurement policies pertaining to the construction and management of federal buildings, disposal of real and personal property, and management of federal property and records. It is also responsible for managing the funding and facilities for former Presidents and presidential transitions.

GSA's real property activities are funded through the Federal Buildings Fund (FBF). The FBF is a revolving fund, into which rental payments from federal agencies that lease GSA space are deposited. Revenue in the fund is then made available by Congress each year to pay for specific activities: construction or purchase of new space, repairs and alterations to existing space, rental payments for space that GSA leases, installment payments, and other building operations expenses. These amounts are referred to as "limitations" because GSA may not obligate more funds from the FBF than permitted by Congress, regardless of how much revenue is available for obligation. Certain debts may also be paid for with FBF funds. A negative total for the FBF occurs when the amount of funds made available for expenditure in a fiscal year is less than the amount of new revenue expected to be deposited. A negative total does not mean that no funds are available from the FBF, only that there is a net gain to the fund under the proposed spending levels.

GSA's operating accounts are funded through direct appropriations, separate from the FBF. The total amount of funding for GSA is calculated by adding the amount of FBF funds made available to the amount of direct appropriations provided. **Table 8** lists the pre-sequester amounts for FY2013, the President's FY2014 request, and amounts recommended by the House and Senate appropriations committees for FY2014.

Table 8. GSA Appropriations, FY2013-FY2014

(in millions of dollars)

Account	FY2013 Pre-sequester	FY2014 Request	FY2014 House Committee	FY2014 Senate Committee	FY2014 Enacted
Federal Buildings Fund	-$1,672	—	-$2,409	—	
Limitations on Availability of Revenue	8,018	9,951	7,541	9,951	
New Construction	*50*	*816*	—	*816*	
Repairs and Alterations	*280*	*1,302*	—	*1,261*	

---

[126] P.L. 105-277.

[127] This section authored by Garrett Hatch (x7-7822).

Account	FY2013 Pre-sequester	FY2014 Request	FY2014 House Committee	FY2014 Senate Committee	FY2014 Enacted
Construction and Repair	—	—	—	*41*	
Capital Projects	—	—	*635*	—	
Installation payments	*127*	*113*	*106*	*113*	
Rental of Space	*5,210*	*5,387*	*4,700*	*5,387*	
Building Operations	*2,351*	*2,331*	*2,100*	*2,331*	
Repayment of Debt	88	—	—	—	
Rental Income to Fund	-9,778	-9,951	-9,951	-9,951	
Operating Accounts	**239**	**248**	**224**	**248**	
Government-wide Policy	61	63	53	63	
Operating Expenses	69	64	63	64	
Office of Inspector General	58	63	68	63	
E-Government Fund	12	20	—	20	
Federal Citizens Services	34	35	—	35	
Former Presidents	4	4	—	4	
Citizen Engagement	—	—	40	—	
Total	**-$1,434**	**$248**	**-$2,185**	**$248**	

Sources: H.Rept. 113-72 and S.Rept. 113-80.

Notes: Figures may not sum due to rounding. "Pre-sequester FY2013" figures are from S.Rept. 113-80 and include across-the-board cuts under the Consolidated and Further Continuing Appropriations Act, 2013 (P.L. 113-6).

As shown in **Table 8**, the President proposed a limit of $9.951 billion from the FBF's available revenue for GSA's real property activities for FY2014. The President also requested $248 million for GSA's operating accounts.

The House Appropriations Committee recommended $7.541 billion from the FBF be made available to GSA for FY2014, $2.410 billion less than the President requested. The House committee also recommended $224 million for GSA's operating accounts, $24 million less than the President requested. The House bill would combine two existing accounts within the FBF, "New Construction" and "Repairs and Alterations" into a single, new account, "Capital Projects." The House bill also specified that, of the $2.1 billion it would provide for building operations, $1.1 billion would be for operating and maintenance expenses and $1.0 billion would be for the salaries and expenses of Public Building Service employees.

The Senate Appropriations Committee recommended the same amounts as the President requested: a limit of $9.951 billion from the FBF for capital projects and $248 million for operating accounts. While the Senate bill's totals matched those of the President's request, the Senate bill would create a new account within the FBF, "Construction and Repair" which would provide $41 million for a single project—the John A. Campbell Courthouse, in Mobile, Alabama.

❀❧⊹❀❀❧⊹❀ ❀❀❧⊹ern❀ ent ❀un❀❧⊹❀❀

Originally unveiled in advance of the President's proposed budget for FY2002, the Electronic Government Fund (E-Gov Fund) and its appropriation historically have been a somewhat contentious matter between the President and Congress. The E-Gov Fund was created to support interagency e-government initiatives approved by the Director of OMB.[129] The fund and the projects it sustains have been closely scrutinized by congressional appropriators and the funding requested and appropriated amounts have varied. For example, the President's initial $20 million request for FY2002 was cut to $5 million. Funding from FY2003 to FY2008 varied from $5 million to $3 million. For FY2009, President George W. Bush requested $5 million for the fund. Congress, however, provided no appropriations.[130] In FY2010, Congress appropriated $34 million, in FY2011, the appropriation dropped to $8 million, and in FY2012 the fund was appropriated $12.4 million

For FY2013, President Obama requested $16.7 million for the E-Gov Fund, $17.3 million (50.9%) less than his FY2012 request.[131] The House and Senate Appropriations Committees recommended the same funding level as the President.[132]

For FY2014, President Obama requested $20.2 million for the E-Gov Fund, which is 20.1% ($3.5 million) more than his FY2013 request—and 40.9% ($13.9 million) less than the $34 million the President requested in FY2012.

For FY2014, the House committee recommended the E-Gov Fund be combined with the Federal Citizen Services Fund[133] and renamed the "Information and Engagement for Citizens" account.[134] The House report indicated: "While these funds were created at different periods of time and

---

[128] This section authored by Wendy Ginsberg (x7-3933).

[129] Pursuant to 44 U.S.C. §3604, the E-Gov Fund projects "may include efforts to make Federal Government information and services more readily available to members of the public (including individuals, businesses, grantees, and State and local governments); make it easier for the public to apply for benefits, receive services, pursue business opportunities, submit information, and otherwise conduct transactions with the Federal Government; and enable Federal agencies to take advantage of information technology in sharing information and conducting transactions with each other and with State and local governments." According to the President's FY2014 budget request, the E-Gov Fund "provides for inter-agency electronic government, or E-Gov, initiatives and projects, which use the Internet or other electronic methods to provide individuals, businesses, and other government agencies with simpler and more timely access to Federal information, benefits, services, and business opportunities." (*The Budget for 2014: Appendix*, p. 1137.)

[130] The E-Gov Fund, in previous years, was not spending its full appropriation.

[131] *Appendix, Budget of the United States, FY2014*, p. 1227.

[132] U.S. Congress, House Committee on Appropriations, *Financial Services and General Government Appropriations Bill, 2013*, report to accompany H.R. 6020, 112th Cong., 2nd sess., June 26, 2012, H.Rept. 112-550 (Washington: GPO, 2013), p. 58; U.S. Congress, Senate Committee on Appropriations, *Financial Services and General Government Appropriations Bill, 2013*, report to accompany S. 3301, 112th Cong., 2nd sess., June 14, 2012, S.Rept. 112-177 (Washington: GPO, 2010), p. 87.

[133] The Federal Citizen Services Fund provides salaries and expenses for the Office of Citizen Services, which "provides citizens, businesses, other governments, and the media with access points to easily obtain Government information and services," U.S. Congress, Senate Committee on Appropriations, *Financial Services and General Government Appropriations Bill, 2011*, report to accompany S. 3677, 111th Cong., 2nd sess., July 29, 2010, S.Rept. 111-238 (Washington: GPO, 2010), p. 98.

[134] A similar recommendation was made, but not enacted, in FY2012.

---

developed different programs, they share a common objective—making it easier for citizens to understand and interact with their government."[135]

If combined, the E-Gov Fund and the Federal Citizen Services Fund were appropriated $46.5 million in FY2013 prior to sequestration. If combined, President Obama requested $55.0 million for the two funds for FY2014. The House committee, however, recommended $40 million for the new, combined fund, which was 27.3% ($15 million) less than the President's FY2014 total request for both funds.

In contrast to the House committee, the Senate committee recommended the E-Gov Fund be appropriated the $20.2 million requested by the President.[136] The Senate report did not address the House's recommendation to merge the E-Gov Fund with the Federal Citizen Services Fund.

Independent Agencies Related to Personnel Management Appropriations

The FSGG appropriations bill includes funding for four agencies with personnel management functions: the Federal Labor Relations Authority (FLRA), the Merit Systems Protection Board (MSPB), the Office of Personnel Management (OPM), and the Office of Special Counsel (OSC). **Table 9** lists the pre-sequester amounts for FY2013, the President's FY2014 request, and amounts recommended by the House and Senate appropriations committees for FY2014, for each of these agencies.

Table 9. Independent Agencies Related to Personnel Management Appropriations, FY2013-FY2014

(in millions of dollars)

Agency	FY2013 Pre-sequester	FY2014 Request	FY2014 House Committee	FY2014 Senate Committee	FY2014 Enacted
Federal Labor Relations Authority (FLRA)	$24.7	$25.5	$24.0	$25.5	
Merit Systems Protection Board (MSPB, total)	42.5	42.4	42.0	45.1	
Salaries and Expenses	*40.2*	*40.1*	*39.7*	*42.7*	
Limitation on Administrative Expenses	*2.3*	*2.3*	*2.3*	*2.3*	
Office of Personnel Management (OPM, total)	20,883	20,875.4	20,871.1	20,875.4	
Salaries and Expenses	*97.6*	*95.8*	*95.6*	*95.8*	
Limitation on Administrative Expenses	*112.3*	*118.6*	*114.5*	*118.6*	
Office of Inspector General	*3.1*	*4.7*	*4.7*	*4.7*	

---

[135] H.Rept. 113-172, p. 59.

[136] S.Rept. 113-80, p. 92.

Agency	FY2013 Pre-sequester	FY2014 Request	FY2014 House Committee	FY2014 Senate Committee	FY2014 Enacted
(OIG, salaries and expenses)					
Office of Inspector General (limitation on administrative expenses)	*21.1*	*21.3*	*21.3*	*21.3*	
Government Payments for Annuitants, Employee Health Benefits	*10,818*	*11,404*	*11,404*	*11,404.0*	
Government Payments for Annuitants, Employee Life Insurance	*51.0*	*53.0*	*53.0⁰*	*53.0*	
Payment to Civil Service Retirement and Disability Fund	*9,780.0*	*9,178.0*	*9,178.0*	*9,178.0*	
Office of Special Counsel (OSC)	$18.9	$20.6	$20.6	$20.6	

Sources: H.Rept. 113-172 and S.Rept. 113-80.

Notes: All figures are rounded, and columns may not equal the total due to rounding. "Pre-sequester FY2013" figures are from S.Rept. 113-80 and include across-the-board cuts under the Consolidated and Further Continuing Appropriations Act, 2013 (P.L. 113-6).

The payments for health benefits, life insurance, and civil service retirement and disability are mandatory appropriations. Appropriations bills have generally provided "such sums as may be necessary" for these accounts and H.R. 2786 and S. 1371 contain this language. For FY2014 (as in FY2012 and FY2013), the House Appropriations Committee did not include funding for these accounts in Title V of the FSGG bill, as it had in previous years and as it appears in the Senate bill. Instead funding for these accounts appears Section 626 of H.R. 2786 (FY2014). In this report, funding for health benefits, life insurance, and retirement is included in Title V to be consistent with prior year calculations.

Federal Labor Relations Authority[137]

The Federal Labor Relations Authority (FLRA) is an independent federal agency that administers and enforces Title VII of the Civil Service Reform Act of 1978.[138] Title VII is also called the Federal Service Labor-Management Relations Statute (FSLMRS). The FSLMRS gives federal employees the right to join or form a union and to bargain collectively over the terms and conditions of employment. Employees also have the right not to join a union that represents employees in their bargaining unit. The statute excludes specific agencies and gives the President the authority to exclude other agencies for reasons of national security. Agencies that are excluded from the statute include the Federal Bureau of Investigation (FBI), Central Intelligence Agency (CIA), Government Accountability Office (GAO), National Security Agency (NSA), Tennessee Valley Authority (TVA), FLRA, Federal Service Impasses Panel (FSIP), and the Secret Service.

The FLRA consists of a three-member authority, the Office of General Counsel, and the FSIP. The three members of the authority and the General Counsel are appointed to five-year terms by the President with the advice and consent of the Senate.

---

[137] This section authored by Gerald Mayer (x7-7815) and Barbara L. Schwemle (x7-8655).
[138] P.L. 95-454.

The authority resolves disputes over the composition of bargaining units, charges of unfair labor practices, objections to representation elections, and other matters. The General Counsel's office conducts representation elections, investigates charges of unfair labor practices, and manages the FLRA's regional offices. The FSIP resolves labor negotiation impasses between federal agencies and labor organizations.

The President's FY2014 budget proposed an appropriation of $25.5 million for the FLRA.

H.R. 2786 as reported by the House Committee on Appropriations would provide an appropriation of $24.0 million for the FLRA, $1.5 million (-5.8%) less than the amount requested by the President.

S. 1371 as reported by the Senate Committee on Appropriations would provide an appropriation of $25.5 million for the FLRA, the same as the President's request, and $1.5 million (+6.2%) more than the amount recommended by the House Appropriations Committee.

Merit Systems Protection Board[139]

The Merit Systems Protection Board (MSPB) is an independent, quasi-judicial agency established to protect the civil service merit system. The MSPB adjudicates appeals primarily involving personnel actions, certain federal employee complaints, and retirement benefits issues.

The President's budget requested an FY2014 appropriation of $42.4 million (including $40.1 million for salaries and expenses) for the MSPB. The agency's FTE employment level was estimated to be 239 for FY2014. MSPB's authorization expired on September 30, 2007.[140]

H.R. 2786 as reported would provide an appropriation of $42.0 million (including $39.7 million for salaries and expenses) for the MSPB which is $415,000 (-1.0%) less than the President's request.

S. 1371 as reported would provide an appropriation of $45.1 million (including $42.7 million for salaries and expenses) for the MSPB, $2.7 million (+6.3%) more than the President's request, and $3.1 million (+7.3%) more than the amount recommended by the House Appropriations Committee.

Office of Personnel Management[141]

The President's budget requested an FY2014 appropriation of $95.8 million for OPM salaries and expenses. This amount included funding of $5.7 million for the Enterprise Human Resources Integration (HRI) project and $1.3 million for the Human Resources Line of Business (HRLOB) project. The budget also requested appropriations of $118.6 million for trust fund transfers; $4.7 million for Office of Inspector General (OIG) salaries and expenses; and $21.3 million for OIG

---

[139] This section authored by Barbara L. Schwemle (x7-8655).

[140] 5 U.S.C. §5509. Legislation (S. 2057, H.R. 3551) was introduced in the 110th Congress that would have reauthorized the MSPB for three years and enhanced the agency's reporting requirements. Legislation to reauthorize the agency was not introduced in the 111th and 112th Congresses and has not been introduced in the 113th Congress.

[141] This section authored by Barbara L. Schwemle (x7-8655).

trust fund transfers for FY2014. The agency's FTE employment level was estimated to be 5,689 for FY2014.

The agency's budget submission stated that the budget "will permit OPM to pursue long-term human resources strategies that deliver results and enhance the values of the civil service," and "permits increased staffing levels ... to maintain timely processing of retirement claims and provide services to annuitants."[142] In addition, it will allow the Office of Inspector General to "continue to advance its prescription drug audit program, which includes audits of pharmacy benefit managers," and to continue the Federal Employees' Health Benefits Program (FEHBP) "claims data warehouse initiative" that "streamlines and enhances the various administrative and analytical procedures involved in the oversight of the FEHBP."[143]

H.R. 2786 as reported would provide appropriations of $95.6 million for OPM salaries and expenses, $114.5 million for trust fund transfers, $4.7 million for OIG salaries and expenses, and $21.3 million for OIG trust fund transfers. These amounts were, respectively, $200,000 (-0.2%) less, $4 million (-3.4%) less, the same, and the same, as the President's request.

Section 626(a)(3), (4), and (5) of H.R. 2786 would provide the mandatory appropriations for the health benefits, life insurance, and retirement accounts. According to the House Committee on Appropriations report, "These are accounts where authorizing language requires the payment of funds." The report stated that the budget request assumed the following estimated costs: $11,404.0 million for the Government Payment for Annuitants, Employee Health Benefits; $53 million for the Government Payment for Annuitants, Employee Life Insurance; and $9,178.0 million for Payment to the Civil Service Retirement and Disability Fund.[144]

The House committee report "encourage[d] Federal agencies to increase recruitment efforts within the United States territories" and directed OPM to provide "monthly reports on its progress in addressing the backlog in [retirement] claims" to the committee.[145]

S. 1371 as reported would provide appropriations of $95.8 million for OPM salaries and expenses, $118.6 million for trust fund transfers, $4.7 million for OIG salaries and expenses, and $21.3 million for OIG trust fund transfers. These amounts were the same as the President's request and, respectively, $200,000 (+0.2%) more, $4 million (+3.5%) more, the same, and the same as the amounts recommended by the House Appropriations Committee.

The Senate report directed OPM "to inform the Committee of developments to improve" the rates for processing retirement claims and "to continue providing reports and status update briefings, as developments and milestones occur, and future plans are determined" for modernization of the retirement records system.[146]

---

[142] *Appendix, Budget of the United States, FY2014,* pp. 1161-1162.

[143] *Appendix, Budget of the United States, FY2014,* p. 1163.

[144] H.Rept. 113-172, p. 121.

[145] H.Rept. 113-172, p. 66.

[146] S.Rept. 113-80, p. 104.

Office of Special Counsel[147]

The President's budget requested an FY2014 appropriation of $20.6 million for the OSC. The agency's FTE employment level was estimated to be 120 for FY2014. The agency's budget submission projected an increase of 14% in the number of whistleblower disclosure, Hatch Act, and prohibited personnel practice cases received. In addition, the agency expected that its "caseload will continue to increase" as a result of enactment of the Whistleblower Protection Act. According to OSC, the requested funding will enable the agency "to implement new mandates from Congress, including the Whistleblower Protection Enhancement Act, protect the employment rights of returning service members, manage historically high intake levels, and protect the federal merit system from prohibited personnel and political practices."[148]

OSC's authorization expired on September 30, 2007.[149]

H.R. 2786 as reported and S. 1371 as reported would both provide an appropriation of $20.6 million for the OSC, the same as the President's request. The Senate report included the committee's acknowledgement that the agency "continues to experience dramatic growth in its caseload and rapid increases in requests for its services."[150]

National Archives and Records Administration[151]

President Obama requested $385.8 million in FY2014 appropriations for the National Archives and Records Administration (NARA),[152] which is $1 million (less than 1%) less than his FY2013 request ($386.8 million)[153] and $17.9 million (4.4%) less than the President's FY2012 request ($403.7 requested in FY2012).[154] Appropriation levels at NARA follow a similar pattern. In FY2012, NARA was appropriated $392.0 million ($11.7 million or 2.9% less than the President's FY2012 budget request). In FY2013, NARA was appropriated $375.0 million ($11.8 million or 3.1% less than the President's FY2013 request), which was reduced to $371 million because of sequester cuts ($15 million or 3.9% less than the FY2013 request).[155]

Operating expenses account for the largest portion of NARA's appropriation request, 96.1% or $370.7 million. As noted, the FY2014 NARA budget request is $1 million less than the FY2013 request. That $1 million was taken from the operating expenses account in FY2014. Some of the reduction in the budget request came from savings related to the operations and maintenance of

---

[147] This section authored by Barbara L. Schwemle (x7-8655).

[148] *Appendix, Budget of the United States, FY2014*, p. 1296.

[149] 5 U.S.C. §5509. The 110th Congress considered, but did not act upon, legislation (S. 2057, H.R. 3551) that would have reauthorized the agency for three years and included provisions to enhance OSC's reporting requirements. Legislation to reauthorize the agency was not introduced in the 111th and 112th Congresses and has not been introduced in the 113th Congress.

[150] S.Rept. 113-80, p. 108.

[151] This section authored by Wendy Ginsberg (x7-3933)

[152] *Appendix, Budget of the United States, FY2014*, p. 1272.

[153] *Appendix, Budget of the United States, FY2014*, p. 1359.

[154] *Appendix, Budget of the United States, FY2014*, p. 1255.

[155] U.S. National Archives and Records Administration, "President Requests $385.8M for National Archives FY 2014 Budget," at http://www.archives.gov/press/press-releases/2013/nr13-86 html.

NARA facilities.[156] Similar to the FY2012 and FY2013 requests, President Obama combined his requests for operating expenses with that for the Electronic Records Archive (ERA) because development of ERA has been largely completed.[157] The President maintained a separate $4.1 million request for the Office of Inspector General (appropriated $4 million in both FY2012 and FY2013), a separate $8.0 million request for repairs and restorations (a 12.1% decrease from the $9.1 million appropriated in both FY2012 and FY2013), and a separate $3.0 million request for the National Historic Publications and Records Commission (NHPRC), which is $2 million (40.0%) less than the $5 million appropriated in both FY2012 and FY2013.[158]

The House committee recommended NARA receive $384.1 million in total appropriations,[159] while the Senate committee recommended $387.8 million.[160] Specifically, the House committee recommended $369.0 million for operating expenses, $1.7 million (less than 1%) less than the President's request of $370.7 million. The Senate committee, however, recommended that NARA receive the President's requested appropriation. In the Senate report to accompany the appropriations bill, the Senate committee referenced a NARA inspector general report that found material weaknesses with NARA's ability to ensure the security of its holdings.[161] Similar to FY2013, the committee included the following language in its report to address concerns related to these weaknesses:

> As the steward of an astronomical volume of temporary and permanent agency records, the Committee strongly urges the Archivist to continue to explore bar-coding and other innovative alternatives for cataloging boxed materials entrusted to NARA's care, institute enhanced quality controls, regain accountability for the security of classified records in its custody, and institute more stringent management controls at the Washington National Records Center and any other facilities in which NARA is the custodian of Federal records.[162]

The Senate committee also commended NARA for its issuance of the Managing Government Records Directive in August 2012. The directive, among other instructions, requires agencies to appoint a senior agency official to oversee records collection and maintenance, and requires agencies to draft a plan that ensures proper retention of electronic records. The committee wrote:

---

[156] *Appendix, Budget of the United States, FY2014*, p. 1272.

[157] *Appendix, Budget of the United States, FY2014*, p. 1273. Appropriation levels for the ERA were reduced in FY2011. In FY2010, the ERA was appropriated $85.5 million. In FY2011, the appropriation was reduced to $71,856,000. The reduction in ERA appropriation levels for FY2011 followed the release of two Government Accountability Office (GAO) reports that raised serious concerns about the implementation of the ERA. One report said that NARA's oversight of the acquisition processes related to creating the Electronic Record Archive had "weaknesses … in most areas." See U.S. Government Accountability Office, *Electronic Records Archive: National Archives Needs to Strengthen Its Capacity to Use Earned Value Techniques to Manage and Oversee Development*, GAO 11-86, January 2011, Highlights, at http://www.gao.gov/new.items/d1186.pdf; and U.S. Government Accountability Office, *Electronic Government: National Archives and Records Administration's Fiscal Year 2011 Expenditure Plan*, GAO 11-299, March 4, 2011, Highlights, at http://www.gao.gov/new.items/d11299.pdf.

[158] *Appendix, Budget of the United States, FY2014*, pp. 1272-1274.

[159] H.Rept. 113-172, p. 63.

[160] S.Rept. 113-80, p. 97.

[161] See, for example, U.S. National Archives and Records Administration Office of Inspector General, "Follow-up Review of OIG Audit Report No. 08-01: Audit of the Process of Safeguarding and Accounting for Presidential Library Artifacts," OIG Audit Report No. 12-10, September 13, 2012, at http://www.archives.gov/oig/pdf/2012/audit-report-12-10.pdf.

[162] S.Rept. 113-80, p. 98.

The Committee urges NARA to continue to explore ways to decrease the risks to Federal records and improve agency records management practices, through inspections, mandatory agency self-assessments, training curricula including on-line courses to reach a broader audience across the Federal Government, and other compliance tools.[163]

The House and Senate Appropriations Committees both recommended that NARA's OIG receive $4.1 million in appropriations, matching the President's budget request.[164] Both committees also recommended that NARA receive $8 million for repairs and restorations, also matching the budget request. The House committee recommended the NHPRC receive $3 million, matching the President's budget request. In contrast, the Senate committee recommended the NHPRC receive $5 million, $2 million (66.7%) more than the budget request. In its report to accompany the appropriations bill, Senate appropriators wrote the following:

> The Committee notes that the funding provided will enable NARA, through the NHPRC, to undertake a variety of initiatives, including advancing archives preservation, access, and digitization projects within the interlocking repositories of historic records and hidden collections; ensuring public access to some of the most important historical resources that are maintained outside of Federal repositories; and digitizing nationally significant historic records collections to facilitate round-the-clock Internet availability.[165]

National Credit Union Administration[166]

The NCUA is an independent federal agency funded largely by the credit unions that the agency charters, insures, and regulates. The NCUA manages the Community Development Revolving Loan Fund Program (CDRLF). Established in 1979, the CDRLF assists officially designated "low-income" credit unions in providing basic financial services to low-income communities. Low-interest loans and deposits are made available to assist these credit unions. Loans or deposits are normally repaid in five years, although shorter repayment periods may be considered. Technical assistance grants are also available to low-income credit unions. Earnings generated from the CDRLF are available to fund technical assistance grants in addition to funds provided for specifically in appropriations acts. Grants are available for improving operations as well as addressing safety and soundness issues.

The President requested, and the Senate Committee on Appropriations recommended, $1.13 million for FY2014, while the House Committee on Appropriations recommended $1.20 million.

Privacy and Civil Liberties Oversight Board[167]

Originally established in 2004 by the Intelligence Reform and Terrorism Prevention Act[168] as an agency within the Executive Office of the President, the Privacy and Civil Liberties Oversight Board (PCLOB) was reconstituted as an independent agency within the executive branch by the

---

[163] S.Rept. 113-80, p. 98.

[164] The House committee recommended NARA's OIG receive $4.1 million, while the Senate committee recommended $4.13 million.

[165] S.Rept. 113-80, p. 100.

[166] This section authored by Darryl Getter (x7-2834).

[167] This section authored by Garrett Hatch (x7-7822).

[168] P.L. 108-458; 118 Stat. 3638.

Implementing Recommendations of the 9/11 Commission Act of 2007.[169] The board assumed its new status on January 30, 2008; its FY2009 appropriation was its first funding as an independent agency. Among its responsibilities, the five-member board is to (1) ensure that concerns with respect to privacy and civil liberties are appropriately considered in the implementation of laws, regulations, and executive branch policies related to efforts to protect the nation against terrorism; (2) review the implementation of laws, regulations, and executive branch policies related to efforts to protect the nation from terrorism, including the implementation of information sharing guidelines; and (3) analyze and review actions the executive branch takes to protect the nation from terrorism, ensuring that the need for such actions is balanced with the need to protect privacy and civil liberties. The board is to advise the President and the heads of executive branch departments and agencies on issues concerning, and findings pertaining to, privacy and civil liberties. The board is to provide annual reports to Congress detailing its activities during the year, and board members appear and testify before congressional committees upon request.

The President requested, and the House Appropriations Committee recommended, $3 million for the PCLOB for FY2014.[170] The Senate Appropriations Committee recommended $4 million for the PCLOB for FY2014, which is $1 million more than the President's FY2014 request.[171]

Recovery Accountability and Transparency Board[172]

The Recovery Accountability and Transparency Board (Recovery Board) was established by the American Recovery and Accountability Act of 2009[173] to provide oversight and transparency in the expenditure of Recovery Act funds. The Recovery Board was funded through the FSGG appropriations bill for the first time in FY2012. In previous fiscal years, the board was funded by a now exhausted Recovery Act appropriation. The President requested $13 million for FY2014. The House and Senate Appropriations Committees both recommended $20 million for the Recovery Board for FY2014, $7 million more than the President's request.[174]

Securities and Exchange Commission[175]

The Securities and Exchange Commission (SEC) administers and enforces federal securities laws to protect investors from fraud, to ensure that sellers of corporate securities disclose accurate financial information, and to maintain fair and orderly trading markets. The SEC's budget is set through the normal appropriations process, but, under the Dodd-Frank Act, the agency's appropriations are offset by fees it collects from securities exchanges on the sales of stock and certain other securities transactions on those exchanges. The collections go directly to the Treasury Department. To achieve the offset, the act requires the agency to adjust the rates of its fees, making the agency's budget deficit-neutral.

---

[169] P.L. 110-53; 121 Stat. 266.

[170] H.Rept. 113-72, p. 142.

[171] S.Rept. 113-80, p. 168.

[172] This section authored by Garrett Hatch (x7-7822).

[173] P.L. 111-5; 123 Stat. 115.

[174] H.Rept. 113-72, p. 142; S.Rept. 113-80, p. 168.

[175] This section authored by Gary Shorter (x7-7772).

For FY2014, the President requested the SEC budget be set at $1.674. The House Appropriations Committee recommended that the agency's FY2014 budget be $1.371 billion. In its report, the committee noted that it "remains concerned that a lack of managerial accountability, focus, prioritization, and internal communication hampers the effectiveness of the SEC."[176]

In S. 1371, the Senate Appropriations Committee recommended that the SEC receive $1.674 billion for FY2014, the same amount requested by the President. In its report on the budget recommendation, the committee observed that its

> recommended funding increase is expected to allow the SEC to more aggressively police the securities markets through examinations and enforcement actions. The resources will help enhance risk-based oversight of the investment management industry, expand inspections of credit rating agencies, and permit the SEC to conduct more comprehensive examinations, reach a broader universe of the entities it regulates, and improve its ability to uncover and prosecute fraud....[177]

The Dodd-Frank Act also established an SEC Reserve Fund to enable the agency to plan for certain long-term expenses, potentially freeing up other funds for agency use in areas such as enforcement and regulation. The Reserve Fund is funded by the agency's traditional collections on registration fees. In any single fiscal year, the SEC may not collect more than $50 million in fees for the reserve fund, and total size of the fund may not exceed more than $100 million. Collections in excess of these amounts are remitted to the Treasury General Fund. Noting that the Reserve Fund is not overseen by Congress and that its use is left to the discretion of the SEC, the House Appropriations Committee argued that the "emergency reserve funds should be used for natural disaster emergencies and other crises, not discretionary priorities within a Federal agency" such as the SEC.[178] As such, the committee recommended, as it also did for FY2013, that the SEC be prohibited from using money in the Reserve Fund during FY2014.

Selective Service System[179]

The Selective Service System (SSS) is an independent federal agency operating with permanent authorization under the Military Selective Service Act.[180] It is not part of the Department of Defense, but its mission is to serve the emergency manpower needs of the military by conscripting personnel when directed by Congress and the President.[181] All males ages 18 through 25 and living in the United States are required to register with the SSS. The induction of men into the military via Selective Service (i.e., the draft) terminated in 1972. In January 1980, President Carter asked Congress to authorize standby draft registration of both men and women. Congress approved funds for male-only registration in June 1980. Efforts are underway to allow women to serve in combat units, which may lead to the modification of registration to include women.[182]

---

[176] H.Rept. 113-72, p. 71.

[177] S.Rept. 113-80, p. 112.

[178] H.Rept. 113-72, p. 70.

[179] This section authored by David Burrelli (x7-8033).

[180] 50 U.S.C. §451 *et seq.*

[181] See http://www.sss.gov/.

[182] On February 15, 2013, H.R. 748 was introduced. A section of this bill would require the registration of women for the Selective Service.

Since 1972, Congress has not renewed any President's authority to begin inducting (i.e., drafting) anyone into the armed services. In 2004, an effort to provide the President with induction authority was rejected.[183]

Funding of the Selective Service System has remained relatively stable over the years in terms of absolute dollars, but has decreased in terms of inflation adjusted funding. For FY2014, the President's request was $24.1 million. The House Appropriations Committee recommended $23.5 million, while the Senate Appropriations Committee recommended $22.9 million.

Small Business Administration[184]

The Small Business Administration (SBA) administers a number of programs intended to assist small firms. Arguably, the SBA's four most important functions are to (1) guarantee loans made by banks and other financial institutions to small businesses—principally through the agency's Section 7(a) and 504/Certified Development Company business loan guaranty programs; (2) make low-interest loans to small businesses, nonprofit organizations, and households that are victims of hurricanes, earthquakes, floods, other physical disasters, and acts of terrorism; (3) finance training and technical assistance programs for small business owners and prospective owners; and (4) serve as an advocate for small business within the federal government.

Prior to sequestration, the SBA was provided an appropriation of $1,849 million in FY2013.[185] Increased funding in FY2013 was provided for disaster assistance related to Hurricane Sandy ($804.0 million) and business loan subsidy costs (an additional $126.5 million). According to the SBA, after sequestration and a required across-the-board rescission, the agency received an appropriation of $1,755 million in FY2013.

According to the SBA, in FY2013, the agency received $437.3 million for salaries and expenses ($414.5 million after sequestration and rescission), $148.0 million for business loan administration ($140.2 million after sequestration and rescission), $337.3 million for business loan subsidy costs ($319.7 million after sequestration and rescission), $896.3 million for disaster loans ($851.2 million after sequestration and rescission), $21.3 million for the Office of the Inspector General ($20.2 million after sequestration and rescission), and $9.1 million for the Office of Advocacy ($8.6 million after sequestration and rescission). In addition, included in the salaries and expense amount was $172.3 million ($155.4 million after sequestration and rescission) for 11 non-credit programs.[186]

---

[183] H.R. 163 in the 108th Congress, October 5, 2004, failed on a vote of 2 Yeas to 402 Nays (Roll Call No. 494).

[184] This section authored by Robert Dilger (x7-3110) and Sean Lowry (x7-9154). For more information see CRS Report RL33243, *Small Business Administration: A Primer on Programs*, by Robert Jay Dilger and Sean Lowry.

[185] Funds appropriated in P.L. 112-74, the Consolidated Appropriations Act, 2012; P.L. 112-175, the Continuing Appropriations Resolution, 2013; and P.L. 113-2, the Disaster Relief Appropriations Act, 2013.

[186] The recommended appropriation amounts in FY2013, prior to sequestration and rescission, for the SBA's non-credit programs were: $112.5 million for Small Business Development Centers, $7.0 million for Service Corps of Retired Executives (SCORE), $14.0 million for Women's Business Centers, $0.998 million for the National Women's Business Council, $20.0 million for Microloan Technical Assistance, $2.5 million for Veterans Business Outreach Centers, $1.25 million for Native American Outreach, $3.1 million for 7(j) Technical Assistance Program, $2.5 million for Historically Underutilized Business Zones (HUBZones), $5.0 million for Regional Innovation Clusters, and $3.5 million for PRIME Technical Assistance. The SBA subsequently decided not to fund the PRIME Technical Assistance program in FY2013 and in FY2014.

The SBA was also approved to provide up to $28.0 billion in small business loan guarantees ($17.5 billion for the 7(a) loan guaranty program, $7.5 billion for the 504/Certified Development Company loan guaranty program, and $3.0 billion for the Small Business Investment Company Program) and up to $12.0 billion for the secondary market guarantee program in FY2013.

For FY2014, President Obama requested $968.8 million for the SBA.[187] The Administration requested $485.9 million for salaries and expenses, $151.6 million for business loan administration, $111.6 million for business loan subsidy costs, $191.9 million for disaster loans, $19.4 million for the Office of the Inspector General, and $8.5 million for the Office of Advocacy. In addition, included in salaries and expenses was a recommended amount of $210.3 million for 14 non-credit programs.[188]

The Administration's proposal would authorize up to $29.0 billion in small business loan guarantees–$17.5 billion for the 7(a) loan guaranty program, $7.5 billion for the 504/Certified Development Company loan guaranty program, and $4.0 billion (an increase from $3.0 billion) for the Small Business Investment Company Program–and up to $12.0 billion for the secondary market guarantee program in FY2014.

The House Committee on Appropriations approved an appropriation of $896.9 million for the SBA for FY2014, $71.9 million less than the Administration's request, of $968.9 million.

The House Committee on Appropriations approved an appropriation of $415.9 million for salaries and expenses, $151.6 million for business loan administration, $111.6 million for business loan subsidy costs, $191.9 million for disaster loans, $17.0 million for the Office of the Inspector General, and $9.0 million for the Office of Advocacy. In addition, the House committee approved, within the salaries and expenses account, $183.9 million for 13 non-credit programs.[189]

The House committee approved up to $29.0 billion in small business loan guarantees ($17.5 billion for the 7(a) loan guaranty program, $7.5 billion for the 504/Certified Development Company loan guaranty program, and $4.0 billion for the Small Business Investment Company Program) and up to $12.0 billion for the secondary market guarantee program in FY2014.

The Senate Committee on Appropriations approved an appropriation of $949.2 million for the SBA for FY2014, a decrease of $900 million from the FY 2013 enacted amount, prior to

---

[187] *Appendix, Budget of the United States, FY2014*, pp. 1175-1186.

[188] The Administration recommended $104.68 million for Small Business Development Centers, $6.52 million for Service Corps of Retired Executives (SCORE), $13.05 million for Women's Business Centers, $0.9 million for the National Women's Business Council, $19.85 million for Microloan Technical Assistance, $2.5 million for Veterans Business Outreach Centers, $1.05 million for Native American Outreach, $2.79 million for 7(j) Technical Assistance Program, $2.0 million for Historically Underutilized Business Zones (HUBZones), $5.0 million for Regional Innovation Clusters, $40.0 million for Entrepreneurship Education, $5.0 million for Growth Accelerators, and $7.0 million for Boots to Business in FY2014. No funding was recommended for the PRIME Technical Assistance Program.

[189] The House Committee on Appropriations recommended an appropriation of $112.5 million for Small Business Development Centers, $7.0 million for Service Corps of Retired Executives (SCORE), $14.0 million for Women's Business Centers, $0.9 million for the National Women's Business Council, $20.0 million for Microloan Technical Assistance, $2.5 million for Veterans Business Development, $1.25 million for Native American Outreach, $2.79 million for 7(j) Technical Assistance Programs, $2.5 million for Historically Underutilized Business Zones (HUBZones), $5.0 million for Entrepreneurial Development Initiative (Clusters), $5.0 million for Entrepreneurship Education, $7.0 million for Boots to Business, and $3.5 million for PRIME Technical Assistance. The House committee did not recommend funding for the Administration's Growth Accelerators Initiative.

sequestration and rescission, of $1,849 million; $19.6 million less than the Administration's recommendation, of $968.8 million; and $52.3 million more than the amount approved by the House committee, of $896.9 million.

The Senate committee approved an appropriation of $254.8 million for salaries and expenses and, separately, $211.5 million for 13 entrepreneurial development (non-credit) programs (for a combined total of $466.3 million),[190] $151.6 million for business loan administration, $111.6 million for business loan subsidy costs, $191.9 million for disaster loans, $19.4 million for the Office of the Inspector General, and $8.5 million for the Office of Advocacy.

The Senate committee approved up to $32.5 billion in small business loan guarantees ($17.5 billion for the 7(a) loan guaranty program, $7.5 billion for the 504/Certified Development Company loan guaranty program, and $7.5 billion for the Small Business Investment Company Program) and up to $12.0 billion for the secondary market guarantee program in FY2014.[191]

United States Postal Service[192]

The U.S. Postal Service (USPS) generates nearly all of its funding—about $65 billion annually—by charging users of the mail for the costs of the services it provides.[193] Congress, however, does provide an annual appropriation to compensate the USPS for revenue it forgoes in providing free mailing privileges to the blind[194] and overseas voters.[195] Congress authorized appropriations for these purposes in the Revenue Forgone Reform Act of 1993 (RFRA).[196] This act also permitted Congress to provide the USPS with a $29 million annual reimbursement until 2035 to pay for the costs of postal services provided at below-cost rates to not-for-profit organizations in the early 1990s.[197] Funds appropriated to the USPS are deposited in the Postal Service Fund, a revolving fund at the U.S. Department of the Treasury.

---

[190] The Senate Committee on Appropriations recommended $114.75 million for Small Business Development Centers, $7.14 million for Service Corps of Retired Executives (SCORE), $14.0 million for Women's Business Centers, $1.0 million for the National Women's Business Council, $20.0 million for Microloan Technical Assistance, $2.5 million for Veterans Business Outreach Centers, $2.0 million for Native American Outreach, $3.1 million for 7(j) Technical Assistance Programs, $2.0 million for Historically Underutilized Business Zones (HUBZones), $5.0 million for Regional Innovation Clusters, $15.0 million for Entrepreneurial Education and Growth Accelerators, $5.0 million for Boots to Business, and $20.0 million for State Trade and Export Promotion (STEP). The Senate committee did not recommend funding for PRIME Technical Assistance.

[191] The Senate Committee on Appropriations also approved the reinstitution of the 504/CDC loan guaranty program's low-interest refinancing program (eligibility beyond business expansions) as previously authorized under P.L. 111-240, the Small Business Jobs Act of 2010, for FY2014.

[192] This section authored by Kevin Kosar (x7-3968). Also see CRS Report RS21025, *The Postal Revenue Forgone Appropriation: Overview and Current Issues*, by Kevin R. Kosar.

[193] U.S. Postal Service, *Annual Report, SEC Form 10K*, November 15, 2012, p. 33. Available at http://about.usps.com/who-we-are/financials/10k-reports/fy2012.pdf.

[194] 84 Stat. 757; 39 U.S.C. §3403. See also USPS, *Mailing Free Matter for Blind and Visually Handicapped Persons: Questions and Answers*, Publication 347 (Washington: USPS, May 2005), available at http://www.usps.com/cpim/ftp/pubs/pub347.pdf.

[195] Members of the Armed Forces and U.S. citizens who live abroad are eligible to register and vote absentee in federal elections under the provisions of the Uniformed and Overseas Citizens Absentee Voting Act of 1986 (42 U.S.C. §1973ff-ff-6). See CRS Report RS20764, *The Uniformed and Overseas Citizens Absentee Voting Act: Overview and Issues*, by Kevin J. Coleman.

[196] P.L. 103-123, Title VII; 107 Stat. 1267; 39 U.S.C. §2401(c)-(d).

[197] See CRS Report RS21025, *The Postal Revenue Forgone Appropriation: Overview and Current Issues*, by Kevin R. (continued...)

The Postal Accountability and Enhancement Act[198] (PAEA), which was enacted on December 20, 2006, first affected the postal appropriations process in FY2009. Under the PAEA, both the U.S. Postal Service Office of Inspector General (USPSOIG) and the Postal Regulatory Commission (PRC) must submit their budget requests directly to Congress and to the Office of Management and Budget.[199] These two agencies must be funded through the Postal Service Fund. The law further requires USPSOIG's budget submission to be treated as part of USPS's total budget, while the PRC's budget, like the budgets of other independent regulators, is treated separately.[200]

For FY2014, the

- USPS and the President requested $70.8 million.[201] The House Appropriations Committee and the Senate Appropriations Committee both recommended this same amount;[202]

- PRC and President requested $14.3 million.[203] The House Appropriations Committee recommended a $14.0 million appropriation, and the Senate Appropriations Committee recommended a $14.3 million appropriation;[204] and

- USPSOIG and the President requested $241.5 million.[205] The House Appropriations Committee recommended $240.0 million, and the Senate Appropriations Committee recommended a $241.5 million appropriation.[206]

Both of the House and Senate FY2014 FSGG measures contain postal policy provisions.

The House FSGG measure would renew four long-standing appropriations policies:

(1) requiring the USPS to continue six-day mail delivery;

(2) stipulating that mail for overseas voting and mail for the blind shall continue to be free;

(3) prohibiting appropriated funds from being used to charge a fee to a child support enforcement agency seeking the address of a postal customer; and

(4) prohibiting funds from being used to consolidate or close small rural and other small post offices.[207]

(...continued)

Kosar.

[198] P.L. 109-435; 120 Stat. 3198. On PAEA's major provisions, see CRS Report R40983, *The Postal Accountability and Enhancement Act of 2006*, by Kevin R. Kosar.

[199] 120 Stat. 3240-3241.

[200] While the PAEA did not authorize any additional appropriations to the Postal Service Fund, it did alter the budget submission process for the USPS's Office of Inspector General (USPSOIG) and the Postal Rate Commission (PRC). In the past, the USPSOIG and the PRC submitted their budget requests to the USPS's Board of Governors. Accordingly, past presidential budgets did not include the USPOIG's or PRC's funding requests or appropriations.

[201] *Appendix, Budget of the United States, FY2014*, p. 1298.

[202] H.Rept. 113-72, p. 77; and S.Rept. 113-80, p. 125.

[203] *Appendix, Budget of the United States, FY2014*, p. 1304.

[204] H.Rept. 113-72, p. 68; and S.Rept. 113-80, p. 108.

[205] *Appendix, Budget of the United States, FY2014*, p. 1303.

[206] H.Rept. 113-72, p. 78; and S.Rept. 113-80, p. 128.

In addition, the House bill would direct the USPS to refrain from selling post offices located in historic properties until the completion of a study by the USPS Office of Inspector General.[208]

The Senate FSGG measure also would renew the same, aforementioned long-standing appropriations policies, such as requiring six-day mail delivery.[209] The Senate bill also would direct the USPS to modify its post office operational hour reduction initiative to reflect the recommendations of the Postal Regulatory Commission.[210] The Senate FSGG bill further would direct the USPS to: expand its retail access in private retail facilities and via self-service kiosks; submit a report to the Senate Appropriations Committee on its efforts to comply with a PRC advisory opinion on mail processing facility closures;[211] and take additional steps before closing any processing facility that has previously been considered for closure. The Senate bill also would direct the GAO to study whether the USPS's "relaxed standards" for delivery have disproportionately affected areas served by alternate means of transportation (AMOT) contracts.[212]

President Obama's FY2014 budget request, like the House and Senate measures, would extend the aforementioned long-standing appropriations policies—except for six-day mail delivery.[213] The Administration also favors

- requiring the Office of Personnel Management to recalculate the USPS's Federal Employee Retirement System balance using USPS's specific demographics, and to return any overpayment to the USPS between FY2014 and FY2015;[214]

- restructuring the USPS's Retiree Health Benefits Fund (RHBF) payments schedule as a 40-year amortization beginning in FY2017; and allowing the USPS to draw upon the RHBF to pay the healthcare insurance premiums for current USPS retirees;[215]

- allowing the USPS to increase collaboration with state and local governments; and

---

(...continued)

[207] H.Rept. 113-72, p. 118.

[208] H.Rept. 113-72, p. 77.

[209] S.Rept. 113-80, pp. 126-128.

[210] Postal Regulatory Commission, "Advisory Opinion On Post Office Structure Plan," Docket No. 2012-2, August 23, 2012, at http://www.prc.gov/Docs/85/85013/N2012-2_Adv_Op_082312.pdf.

[211] Postal Regulatory Commission, "Advisory Opinion On Mail Processing Network Rationalization Service Changes," Docket No. 2012-2, September 28, 2012, at http://www.prc.gov/Docs/85/85269/ Advisory_Opinion_%20PDF%20_09282012.pdf.

[212] U.S. Postal Service, "Revised Service Standards for Market-Dominant Mail Products," 77 *Fed□a□□egiste□*31190, May 25, 2012, at https://www.federalregister.gov/articles/2012/05/25/2012-12564/revised-service-standards-for-market-dominant-mail-products.

[213] *Appendix, Budget of the United States, FY2014*, pp. 1298-1299.

[214] *Appendix, Budget of the United States, FY2014*, p. 1302.

[215] Current law provides for 10 years of fixed payments followed by a 40-year amortization of any remaining unfunded obligation. Current law also forbids drawing funds from the RHBF until FY2017. *Appendix, Budget of the United States, FY2014*, pp. 1166-1167.

- permitting the USPS to enact a one-time postage increase beyond the current postage rate cap.[216]

"All together," the *Budget* stated, "these reforms would provide USPS with over $30 billion in cash relief, operational revenue, and produce PAYGO savings of over $23 billion over the next over 11 years."[217]

United States Tax Court[218]

A court of record under Article I of the Constitution, the United States Tax Court (USTC) is an independent judicial body that has jurisdiction over various tax matters as set forth in Title 26 of the United States Code. The court is headquartered in Washington, DC, but its judges conduct trials in many cities across the country.

The USTC received $51 million in FY2013. The President requested $53 million for FY2014. The House Appropriations Committee recommended $51 million for FY2014, which would be $2 million less than the President's request.[219] The Senate Appropriations Committee recommended $53 million for FY2014, the same as the President requested and $2 million above the FY2013 enacted amount.[220]

General Provisions Government-Wide[221]

The Financial Services and General Government Appropriations Act includes general provisions applying government-wide. Most of the provisions continue language that has appeared under the General Provisions title for several years because Congress has decided to reiterate the language rather than making the provisions permanent. An Administration's proposed government-wide general provisions for a fiscal year are generally included in the Budget Appendix.[222] New provisions proposed in the FY2014 budget follow. These provisions were not included in H.R. 2786 as reported or S. 1371 as reported except as otherwise noted.

New Government-wide General Provisions Proposed for FY2014

- Section 732 of the President's proposed budget would prohibit a pay raise in calendar year 2013, for the Vice President, and in calendar year 2014, for a political appointee serving in an Executive Schedule position, or in a position for which the rate of pay is fixed by statute at an Executive Schedule rate; a chief of mission or ambassador at large; a noncareer appointee in the Senior Executive Service; and a political appointee paid a rate of basic pay (including locality-

---

[216] By law (39 U.S.C. §3622(d)(1)(A)), the USPS may raise rates on most of its products and services no higher than the rate of inflation.

[217] *Appendix, Budget of the United States, FY2014*, pp. 1302.

[218] This section authored by Garrett Hatch (x7-7822).

[219] H.Rept. 113-72, p. 143.

[220] S.Rept. 113-80, p. 169.

[221] This section authored by Barbara L. Schwemle (x7-8655).

[222] For FY2014, the provisions are listed in the *Appendix, Budget of the United States, FY2014*, pp. 9-12.

based payments) at or above level IV of the Executive Schedule. Included in S. 1371 as reported at Section 742.

- Section 733 of the President's proposed budget would prohibit the use of funds appropriated, in this or any other act, for FY2014, to provide a pay adjustment to federal blue-collar employees that exceeds: (1) the rate payable for the applicable grade and step of the applicable wage schedule during the period from the date of expiration of the limitation imposed by the comparable section for previous fiscal years until the normal effective date of the applicable wage survey adjustment that is to take effect in FY2014; and (2) as a result of a wage survey adjustment, the rate payable under paragraph (1) by more than the sum of (A) the General Schedule pay adjustment for FY2014 and (B) the difference between the overall average percentage of the locality-based comparability payments taking effect in FY2014, and the overall average percentage of such payments which was effective in the previous fiscal year under such section, during the remainder of FY2014. Included in Section 741 of S. 1371 as reported.

- Section 734 of the President's proposed budget would provide that funds made available and used for Pay for Success projects in this or any other act would support performance-based awards that are designed to promote innovative strategies to reduce the aggregate level of government investment needed to achieve successful outcomes. The awards would impose minimal administrative requirements on service providers to allow for maximum flexibility to improve efficiency and effectiveness. The OMB Director would issue guidance to federal agencies on carrying out such projects. (This provision was also proposed by the Administration in the FY2012 and FY2013 budget requests, but was not enacted.)

- Section 735 of the President's proposed budget would require the OMB Director to report to the House and Senate Committees on Appropriations on at least a quarterly basis on the status of unexpired, unobligated balances of budget authority in executive branch agencies. The reports would, to the extent practicable, separately identify such budget authority for discretionary appropriations and direct spending. With regard to such budget authority for discretionary appropriations, the reports would, to the extent practicable, separately identify those balances that are available to fund reimbursable obligations and all other balances of discretionary budget authority. The reports would be submitted not later than 30 days after the end of a fiscal quarter.

H.R. 2786 as reported included the following new general provisions (which were not included in S. 1371 as reported).

- Section 736 of H.R. 2786 as reported would prohibit the use of appropriated funds for the painting of a portrait of an employee of the Federal government including the President, the Vice President, a Member of Congress, the head of an executive branch agency, or the head of an office of the legislative branch.

- Section 738 of H.R. 2786 as reported would prohibit the use of appropriated funds to pay more than 75% of the salary of the Commissioner and any Deputy Commissioner of Internal Revenue if the Internal Revenue Service agency does not comply with certain Inspector General recommendations by July 1, 2014.

Cuba Sanctions[223]

As reported by the Appropriations committees, H.R. 2786 and S. 1371 have different provisions regarding U.S. policy regarding travel to Cuba. The House version would tighten restrictions on travel by prohibiting funding for any additional authorization of people-to-people exchanges during the fiscal year, while the Senate version would ease restrictions on travel by authorizing a new general license for professional travel related to disaster prevention, emergency preparedness, and natural resource protection.

Restrictions on travel to Cuba have been a key and often contentious component of U.S. efforts to isolate Cuba's communist government for much of the past 50 years. Over time there have been numerous changes to the restrictions and for five years, from 1977 until 1982, there were no restrictions on travel. Restrictions on travel to Cuba are part of the Cuban Assets Control Regulations (CACR), the overall embargo regulations administered by the Treasury Department's Office of Foreign Assets Control (OFAC). First issued in 1963, the CACR have been amended many times over the years to reflect changes in policy, and remain in force today. In 2009, the Obama Administration eased restrictions for family travel, and in 2011 the Administration further eased travel restrictions for religious and educational activities, including people-to-people travel.

At present, eight categories of travelers may travel to Cuba under a *general* license, which means that there is no need to obtain special permission from OFAC. This includes those visiting close relatives in Cuba; full-time journalists; full-time professionals conducting professional research (of a noncommercial, academic nature) or attending conferences sponsored by international professional organizations or associations; faculty, staff, and students of accredited U.S. graduate and undergraduate degree-making institutions engaged in educational activities; members and staff of religious organizations engaged in a full-time program of religious activities; and travel related to licensed sales of agricultural, medical, and telecommunications products. In addition, 15 categories of travelers engaging in a variety of activities, including educational, religious, and humanitarian activities and people-to-people exchanges may be eligible for *specific* licenses. Applications for *specific* licenses are reviewed and granted by OFAC on a case-by-case basis. The specific licenses for people-to-people travel are generally issued for one year to organizations that sponsor and organize such trips.

As reported by the House committee, H.R. 2786 includes a provision in Section 124 that would prohibit FY2014 funding used "to approve, license, facilitate, authorize, or otherwise allow" travel-related or other transactions related to nonacademic educational exchanges (i.e., people-to-people travel) to Cuba set forth in 31 CFR 515.565(b)(2) of the CACR. The committee report to the House bill contends that this category of travel violates the prohibition on travel related to tourist activities set forth in the Trade Sanctions Reform and Export Enhancement Act of 2000.[224] The report also maintains that the stated purpose of people-to-people travel—to promote the Cuban people's independence from Cuban authorities—"cannot be accomplished through itineraries that mainly feature interactions with representatives of a dictatorship that actively oppresses the Cuban people, nor can it be accomplished through itineraries that do not require

---

[223] This section authored by Mark P. Sullivan (x7-7689). For additional information, see CRS Report R43024, *Cuba: U.S. Policy and Issues for the 111th Congress*, by Mark P. Sullivan, and CRS Report RL31139, *Cuba: U.S. Restrictions on Travel and Remittances*, by Mark P. Sullivan http://www.crs.gov/pages/Reports.aspx?PRODCODE=RL31139.

[224] P.L. 106-387, Title IX.

meetings with pro-democracy activists or independent members of Cuban civil society." In contrast, the Obama Administration has defended such travel, maintaining that it helps build connections between the Cuban and American people in order to give Cubans the support and tools they need to move forward independent of the government. According to Assistant Secretary of State for Western Hemisphere Affairs Roberta Jacobson, "the Administration's travel, remittance and people-to-people policies are helping Cubans by providing alternative sources of information, taking advantage of emerging opportunities for self-employment and private property, and strengthening civil society."[225]

The House bill has a second Cuba provision in Section 125 that would require a Treasury Department report within 90 days of the bill's enactment with information for each fiscal year since FY2007 on the number of travelers visiting close relatives in Cuba; the average duration of these trips; the average amount of U.S. dollars spent per family traveler (including amount of remittances carried to Cuba); the number of return trips per year; and the total sum of U.S. dollars spent collectively by family travelers for each fiscal year.

As reported by the Senate committee, S. 1371 includes a provision in Section 628 that would provide for a new general license for travel-related transactions for full-time professional research; for attendance at professional meetings if the sponsoring organization is a U.S. organization; and for the organization and management of professional meetings and conferences in Cuba if the sponsoring organization is a U.S. professional organization if the travel is related to disaster prevention, emergency preparedness, and natural resource protection, including for fisheries, coral reefs, and migratory species. This provision would expand the current general licenses available for professional research and meetings in Cuba that allow full-time professionals to conduct professional research in their areas (with certain conditions), attend professional meetings or conferences in Cuba organized by an international professional organization, and attend professional meetings for commercial telecommunications transactions (31 CFR 515.564).

---

[225] Testimony of Roberta S. Jacobson, Assistant Secretary of State for Western Hemisphere Affairs, in U.S. Congress, Senate Committee on Foreign Relations, Subcommittee on Western Hemisphere, Peace Corps and Global Narcotics Affairs, *The Path to Freedom: Countering Depression and Strengthening Civil Society*, 112th Cong., 2nd sess., June 7, 2012; available at http://www.state.gov/p/wha/rls/rm/2012/191935 htm.

Key Policy Staff

Area of Expertise	Name	Phone	E-mail
Department of the Treasury	Gary Guenther	7-7742	gguenther@crs.loc.gov
Executive Office of the President	Barbara L. Schwemle	7-8655	bschwemle@crs.loc.gov
Judiciary	Matt Glassman	7-3467	mglassman@crs.loc.gov
District of Columbia	Eugene Boyd	7-8689	eboyd@crs.loc.gov
Commodity Futures Trading Commission	Rena Miller	7-0826	rsmiller@crs.loc.gov
Election Assistance Commission	Kevin Coleman	7-7878	kcoleman@crs.loc.gov
E-Government Fund in GSA	Wendy Ginsberg	7-3933	wginsberg@crs.loc.gov
Executive Office of the President	Barbara Schwemle	7-8655	bschwemle@crs.loc.gov
Federal Communications Commission	Patty Figliola	7-2508	pfigliola@crs.loc.gov
Federal Deposit Insurance Corporation	Darryl Getter	7-2834	dgetter@crs.loc.gov
Federal Election Commission	R. Sam Garrett	7-6443	rgarrett@crs.loc.gov
Federal Labor Relations Authority	Gerald Mayer	7-7815	gmayer@crs.loc.gov
Federal Trade Commission	Gary Guenther	7-7742	gguenther@crs.loc.gov
General Services Administration	Garrett Hatch	7-8674	ghatch@crs.loc.gov
Merit Systems Protection Board	Barbara Schwemle	7-8655	bschwemle@crs.loc.gov
National Archives and Records Administration	Wendy Ginsberg	7-3933	wginsberg@crs.loc.gov
National Credit Union Administration	Darryl Getter	7-2834	dgetter@crs.loc.gov
Office of Personnel Management	Barbara Schwemle	7-8655	bschwemle@crs.loc.gov
Office of Special Counsel	Barbara Schwemle	7-8655	bschwemle@crs.loc.gov
Securities and Exchange Commission	Gary Shorter	7-7772	gshorter@crs.loc.gov
Selective Service System	David Burrelli	7-8033	dburrelli@crs.loc.gov
Small Business Administration	Robert Dilger	7-3110	rdilger@crs.loc.gov
Small Business Administration	Sean Lowry	7-9154	slowry@crs.loc.gov
U.S. Postal Service	Kevin Kosar	7-3968	kkosar@crs.loc.gov
Government-wide General Provisions	Barbara Schwemle	7-8655	bschwemle@crs.loc.gov
Competitive Sourcing	L. Elaine Halchin	7-0646	ehalchin@crs.loc.gov
Cuba	Mark Sullivan	7-7689	msullivan@crs.loc.gov

Author Contact Information

Baird Webel, Coordinator
Specialist in Financial Economics
bwebel@crs.loc.gov, 7-0652

Eugene Boyd
Analyst in Federalism and Economic Development
Policy
eboyd@crs.loc.gov, 7-8689

David F. Burrelli
Specialist in Military Manpower Policy
dburrelli@crs.loc.gov, 7-8033

Kevin J. Coleman
Analyst in Elections
kcoleman@crs.loc.gov, 7-7878

Robert Jay Dilger
Senior Specialist in American National Government
rdilger@crs.loc.gov, 7-3110

Patricia Moloney Figliola
Specialist in Internet and Telecommunications
Policy
pfigliola@crs.loc.gov, 7-2508

R. Sam Garrett
Specialist in American National Government
rgarrett@crs.loc.gov, 7-6443

Darryl E. Getter
Specialist in Financial Economics
dgetter@crs.loc.gov, 7-2834

Wendy Ginsberg
Analyst in American National Government
wginsberg@crs.loc.gov, 7-3933

Matthew E. Glassman
Analyst on the Congress
mglassman@crs.loc.gov, 7-3467

Gary Guenther
Analyst in Public Finance
gguenther@crs.loc.gov, 7-7742

L. Elaine Halchin
Specialist in American National Government
ehalchin@crs.loc.gov, 7-0646

Garrett Hatch
Specialist in American National Government
ghatch@crs.loc.gov, 7-7822

Kevin R. Kosar
Acting Section Research Manager and Analyst in
American and National Government
kkosar@crs.loc.gov, 7-3968

Sean Lowry
Analyst in Public Finance
slowry@crs.loc.gov, 7-9154

Gerald Mayer
Analyst in Labor Policy
gmayer@crs.loc.gov, 7-7815

Barbara L. Schwemle
Analyst in American National Government
bschwemle@crs.loc.gov, 7-8655

Gary Shorter
Specialist in Financial Economics
gshorter@crs.loc.gov, 7-7772

Mark P. Sullivan
Specialist in Latin American Affairs
msullivan@crs.loc.gov, 7-7689

www.ingramcontent.com/pod-product-compliance
Lightning Source LLC
Chambersburg PA
CBHW081835170526
45167CB00007B/2816